Ecotourism Development in Costa Rica

Ecotourism Development in Costa Rica

The Search for Oro Verde

Andrew P. Miller

LEXINGTON BOOKS
Lanham • Boulder • New York • Toronto • Plymouth, UK

Published by Lexington Books
A wholly owned subsidary of Rowman & Littlefield
4501 Forbes Boulevard, Suite 200, Lanham, Maryland 20706
www.rowman.com

16 Carlisle Street, London W1D 3BT, United Kingdom

British Library Cataloguing in Publication Information Available

Library of Congress Cataloging-in-Publication Data

The hardback edition of this book was previously
catalogued by the Library of Congress as follows:

Miller, Andrew P., 1961-
Ecotourism development in Costa Rica : the search for oro verde I Andrew P. Miller.
    p. cm.
    Includes bibliographical references.
I. Ecotourism-Costa Rica. 2. Sustainable Tourism-Costa Rica I. Title. GI56.5.E26 M53
2012
338.4'7917286-dc23   2012018300

ISBN 978-0-7391-7460-9 (cloth : alk. paper)
ISBN 978-0-7391-9725-7 (pbk. : alk. paper)
ISBN 978-0-7391-7461-6 (electronic)

Printed in the United States of America

Dedicated to the memory of Arthur Redmond (1984–2008).
Be excellent to each other.

Contents

Tables

Acknowledgments

Writing this book has been one of the most challenging and rewarding things I have ever done and it would not have been possible without the help of many great people. I am especially grateful to the University of Pittsburgh for the financial support during the beginning stages of this project. I have also been supported by a number of grants from Wilkes University, which facilitated the writing of this book.

Ever since the idea for this book occurred to me on the front porch of my bungalow at La Posada near Manuel Antonio, I have traveled to Costa Rica many times in support of my research and I would like to thank all of the Ticos who have assisted me along the way in understanding their country. A major part of the inspiration for this book has been seeing the progress that Costa Rica has made over the last few decades and the effect that this has had on the Costa Rican standard of living. In particular, I owe a debt of gratitude to Kattya Lomel for dragging groups of students and I wherever we wanted to go and opening so many doors along the way. I would also like to thank Félix Monge at Coopetarrazú for patiently and with great cheer answering my seemingly endless questions. I am very fortunate to be able to count Kattya and Félix among my friends.

I would also like to thank my students at Wilkes University—especially the various groups that have participated in ASB-Costa Rica. Your excitement about service work in Costa Rica has been a strong motivation to finishing this book and each year that I take a new group I get to experience Costa Rica through your eyes. I would also like to thank all of my classes that have been forced to listen to various ideas found in this book, some of them more than once— without you many of these ideas would not be nearly as well developed. It is also important to mention that without Megan Boone Valkenburg, much of what is mentioned above would not have been possible.

Thanks to Mark Harris for the many times he read and reread this manuscript pointing out various improvements along the way, this book is much better thanks to him.

I would also like to thank "The Boulevard" for helping to keep me sane throughout the long process of writing this book. Most of all I would like to thank my wife, Christy, for all her support during this project. Like many things in my life, I could never have done it without her. This book is dedicated to the memory of Art Redmond.

Although each of these people contributed to the final product, any errors contained in this book are mine alone.

Introduction
What Is Ecotourism?

Costa Ricans have long had a close relationship with the land; whether it is the farmers of Tarrazú tending their coffee bushes or the ecotourism guide taking tourists on a walking tour of Manuel Antonio Park, many Costa Ricans make their livelihood from the natural environment. Costa Rica's relationship with the land has also helped to create a very unique societal mind-set among its population regarding the need for conservation and sustainability. Since the 1980s, Costa Rica has become imbued with an extraordinary society-wide environmental ethic that has helped to inform the decision-making processes of a large segment of the population as well as many politicians. In the same way that the abolition of the military helped to foster a society-wide nonviolent ethic, the preservation of the natural world has helped to place environmentalism at the center of the Costa Rican national consciousness. Despite its status as a developing country, Costa Rica is widely seen as a world leader in ecotourism as well as in environmental policy, which includes its goal to be the first carbon neutral country in the world by 2021. One of the most important figures in this movement has been former Costa Rican president Óscar Arias, who acknowledged a symbiotic relationship between long-term economic growth and environmental protection and cites Costa Rica's ongoing experiences with environmental tourism, eco-agriculture, debt for nature swaps, and national park systems as a way to reduce poverty through environmentally sustainable development.[1]

One of the most unique manifestations of Costa Rican environmental consciousness is the focus on ecotourism and its use as a strategy for national development. Endowed with magnificent and diverse natural treasures, Costa Rica was one of the first countries to realize the potential of the notion of "ecotourism," which was first used by a marketing agency attempting to promote Costa Rica as a rain forest destination in the early 1970s.[2] Since then, ecotourism in Costa Rica has grown rapidly and now represents one of the country's most important sources of foreign exchange. Ecotourism in Costa Rica has also been facilitated by the

1

effects of globalization including the relative ease of international travel and the rise of modern communication systems. These factors have helped to facilitate travel to what had once been considered "far-flung" parts of the globe. The increased growth in travel to the developing world led the United Nations Environmental Programme (UNEP) to find that "proportionately, tourism will grow faster in less developed countries than in developed economies in the next ten years."[3]

The ease of communication and travel as well as the cessation of the region's civil wars has helped Costa Rica to attract tourists and its attractions are routinely ranked by travel guides as some of the best in the world. Among the most famous places to visit are Arenal Volcano, Manuel Antonio Park and Monteverde Cloud Forest. The single largest factor that attracts tourists to Costa Rica is the country's exceptional level of biodiversity, all of which is packed into a very small country. While Costa Rica accounts for only 19,600 square miles of territory, it contains more species of plants and animals than the United States and Canada combined. In total, Costa Rica offers 850 species of birds, 220 species of reptiles, 160 species of amphibians, 280 species of mammals, and 130 species of freshwater fish, and 9000 species of plants.[4] These factors prompted *The Daily Mail* (UK) to declare Costa Rica the "perfect destination for adventure seekers, wildlife fans, and lovers of rolling green hills."[5]

Due to its biodiversity and varied ecosystems, most ecotourists engage in activities that are in some way connected to the environment. According to exit polling data from the Instituto Costarricense de Turismo (ICT), Table 1.1 shows the top ten activities of tourists on their trip.

Table 1.1: Top Ten Activities of Tourists

Activity	Percent of Visitors Who Did the Activity, 2010
Go to the beach	68.8%
Observe plants and animals	53.5%
Walk on nature trails	53.1%
Visit a volcano	49.4%
Shopping	41.5%
Bird watching	41.2%
Zip lining	41.0%
Visit hot springs	29.6%
Bungee jumping	17.8%
Surfing	17.3%

Source: ICT, via www.visitcostarica.com, poll given to outgoing tourists from Juan Santamaria Airport, San José

The desire to take an ecologically based vacation also coincides with what Frank, Hironaka, and Schofer[6] refer to as the global institutionalization of environmentalism, which has led to an increase in activities to protect the natural environment in response to a global redefinition of environmental stewardship for the nation-state as well as a burgeoning awareness among regular citizens of the ecological impact of their personal choices. Frank argues that the rise of environment awareness in world society is due in part to a reconstitution of "nature" away from a realm of chaos and a cornucopia of "resources" toward conceptions of nature as a universal, life-sustaining "environment" or ecosystem.[7] The combination of interest in and reorientation toward the environment coupled with the ease of global travel all make ecotourism an appealing possibility for long-term economic development.

What Is Ecotourism?

People have engaged in tourism activities for millennia. The ancient Romans, for instance, would document all of the places they had visited by carving the locations onto their tombstones. In the nineteenth century, the advent of railroads facilitated tourism by making longer trips feasible, thus enabling the newly formed middle-class to spend a portion of their income on leisure activities. In the last two decades, advances in modern air travel have made much of the world accessible to a large portion of the developed world and have made many tropical destinations such as Jamaica, Bermuda, or Cancún common destinations for a large number of tourists. The tourism activities at these destinations are typically centered on large resorts disconnected from the local population and culture and serve largely as enclaves of North American culture. As larger and larger numbers of tourists began to travel, it became clear that large-scale mass tourism played a role in a host of problems related to the overuse of resources and damage to the environment while providing very limited economic benefit to the local population. Cancún, known among locals as *Gringolandia* due to the large number of Americans who visit, has become so disconnected from local people and culture that:

> Cancún has become a simulacrum—an artificial reproduction and representation of the Yucatan physical environment and Maya heritage manifest in a constructed physical and cultural landscape—and the result is Gringolandia, a dynamic 'hybrid-space' in which elements of Mexican, American, and artificial Maya culture have been reconstituted for tourist consumption.[8]

Bhatt and Liyakhat[9] argue that the concept of ecotourism came into being due to the recognition of the ill effects of mass tourism and the need to develop a form of tourism that was sensitive to the environment and could provide economic benefit to the local population. As the negative aspects of mass tourism became clear, many people began to look for an alternative, and the idea of ecotourism was born. When ecotourism emerged on the world tourism market, it did so under a series of more or less accurate names such as adventure tourism, pro-poor tourism, or geotourism, with the frequent use of the terms "responsible," "sustainable," "green," or "low impact."[10] Due to the myriad buzzwords used to describe ecotourism and the broad spectrum of possible activities it encompasses, its exact definition as well as exactly what it entails have long been in dispute. Problems of definition are also due to the travel industry's desire to tap into environmentalism as a money-making device, thus deeming nearly any activity done outdoors as ecotourism, even going so far as to include Sunday afternoon drives.[11] In the last decade or so, scholars and ecotourism organizations have begun to arrive at definitions of ecotourism that include most of these characteristics; travel to natural destinations, the need for conservation and sustainability with local control and significant portions of the revenue kept within the local community that the tourists have visited.

The International Ecotourism Society (IES) defines ecotourism as "responsible travel to natural areas that conserves the environment and improves the well-being of local people by creating an international network of individuals, institutions and the tourism industry and by educating tourists and tourism professionals, influencing the tourism industry, public institutions and donors to integrate the principles of ecotourism into their operations and policies."[12] The most widely accepted and comprehensive definition of ecotourism is provided by Martha Honey and joins together economic, political and social characteristics with environmental concerns. For Honey, ecotourism has the following characteristics:

1.   Involves travel to natural destinations.
2.   Minimizes impact.
3.   Builds environmental awareness.
4.   Provides direct financial benefits for conservation.
5.   Provides financial benefits and empowerment for local people.
6.   Respects local culture.
7.   Supports human rights and democratic movements.[13]

Honey further condenses these characteristics into a holistic definition of ecotourism. "Ecotourism is travel to fragile, pristine, and usually protected areas that strives to be low impact and (often) small scale. It helps educate the traveler, provides funds for conservation, directly benefits the economic development and political empowerment of local communities and fosters respect for different cultures and for human rights."[14] Since ecotourism was created in part as an alternative to mass tourism, many ecotourism advocates contrast ecotourism with mass tourism, which is "typified by the package tour in which itineraries are fixed, stops are planned and guided, and all major decisions are left to the organizer. Familiarity is at a maximum and novelty at a minimum and the safety and companionship gained from traveling with others is paramount."[15] Traditional mass tourism has also served as a motivation for more socially aware ecotourists particularly those who feel "alienated by the increasingly commercialized resort which loses its exotic, idiosyncratic charm for them."[16]

Ecotourism, on the other hand, tends to be much more experientially diffuse, closer to nature and more concerned with simple and sustainable practices and accommodations. Ecotourism also tends to lead travelers to places that are not often considered to be part of the typical tourist trail, a key aspect for those tired of the usual big resort tourism. As a result, ecotourists tend to be more concerned with forming a connection with the local culture, simplicity, and opportunities for learning rather than the pursuit of luxurious accommodations and pampering. Chan and Baum found that "ecotourists interpret ecotourism experiences in association with nature and the environment, simple accommodation and facilities, and a learning experience."[17]

Due to the differences between ecotourism and traditional mass tourism, ecotourism tends to attract older, more educated tourists who are willing to spend more money in order to have a unique and educational experience. Zografos and Allcroft found the profile of an ecotourist to be a person who is typically between thirty-five and fifty-four years of age, willing to spend more money on an eco-tourism trip than a standard vacation, wants to spend between one and two weeks away and states his/her motivations for the trip as a desire to enjoy scenery and nature and to experience new places, with a large proportion who are members of an environmental charity or organization.[18] In addition, Epler Wood found that a large majority of ecotourists are college graduates.[19] The combination of exotic locales and the ecotourist's desire to travel outside "the bubble" of mass tourism, coupled with the inherent social dimensions of ecotourism, means that they place "value on the distinct perspectives of the local inhabitants and an educational process that is multidirectional, experiential, and applied."[20]

The high percentage of college-educated ecotourists who select a destination based on their interest in conservation is not only emblematic of the reorientation toward environmental awareness over the last few decades, but also creates a unique opportunity to further educate people on ecologically sustainable practices beyond basic ideas like recycling and to help them understand the full breadth of environmental issues inherent in the footprint of many tourism businesses:

> If you were to randomly select a skier from an Aspen slope and ask him or her what ski resorts and skiers should be doing to protect the environment, the answer would be "recycle." In ASC's experience, the absence of recycling containers in any area guarantees guest and employee complaints. Many ski-area managers have the same perspective: "environmentalism = recycling." Taken a step further, conventional environmental thinking in the guest-service industry leads to "don't wash my towels" signs and unsophisticated environmental education efforts. Although these measures are important, they miss the bulk of the industry's ecological footprint. And they are, often intentionally, a denial of the real issues.[21]

For scholars such as Ceballos-Lascurain[22] and Stem et al.,[23] the key attribute of ecotourism is the education of ecotourists. Ecotourism has the unique ability to educate because ecotourists are a captive audience who have opted into their excursion presumably based on a shared interest in experiencing the flora and fauna of their destination. As Giannecchini points out "tourists and parks hold the potential to form a perfect partnership to nurture ecological literacy: a captive, self-declared audience in an outdoor, natural setting."[24] As a result of an ecotourist's interest in being educated, Orams found that the more explicit the educational component, the more likely it was to actually change behavior since "tourists who were given the education program became significantly more 'green' in their behavior."[25] The learning inherent in ecotourism also means that people will seek out ecotourism vacations due to their own interest in the environment and will return home with a better grasp of ecological issues and potentially different perspectives concerning changed behaviors toward the environment.

One of the key components for ecotourism to successfully educate its customers is a talented and knowledgeable guide. Not only is an excellent guide good business, but it also serves to enhance the experience of ecotourists and can even imbue them with a better environmental ethic. Peake, Innes, and Dyer found that an effective ecotourism guide can play a role in conservation that is important both to business and natural resource sustainability.[26] As people have become more interested in ecotourism and environmental issues, ecotourism's focus on education has even begun to spawn a subset of activities known as "research ecotourism" for those whose ecotourism trip is planned within a research-oriented framework with activities directed toward conservation, monitoring of the natural environment, and sustainable community development.[27]

If ecotourism is to provide a sustainable source of continuing income for the developing world it is important for ecotourism businesses to embrace the burgeoning environmental ethic, but to do so in an authentic way. There is building evidence that ecotourists desire authentic environmental standards, not just lip service to environmentalism. For instance, Andereck found that not only is nature a motivator for tourism, but tourists place fairly high levels of importance and value on environmentally friendly practices and tourism and recreation sites and businesses.[28] In a study of Manuel Antonio Park in Costa Rica, Cotrell et al. found that "tourists are sensitive towards sustainability issues and judge the ecological dimensions of sustainability related to tourism as the most important."[29] The extent to which socially aware ecotourists can have their desire for sustainability met by ecotourism businesses is the key to future sustainability and maintenance of ecotourism. While tapping into something that looks like ecotourism is most likely quite simple, doing so in an authentic and sustainable manner proves to be more difficult.

While acknowledging the importance of each aspect of ecotourism, this book will focus on issues of local empowerment leading to economic development and measures to increase sustainability. These components of ecotourism are the most important initial steps in improving the lives of people throughout the developing world. Sustainability is a necessary first step to any kind of long-range development plan and will help to increase environmental awareness while economic development will help to bring about changes that will lead to the other goals of ecotourism such as financial benefits for conservation and a democratic movement that will support the promotion of human rights. Finally, the educational aspects of ecotourism and the sort of people who choose ecotourism will inevitably lead to respect for local culture.

Ecotourism as Development Strategy

Ecotourism is attractive as a development strategy not only because of its focus on a broad range of issues ranging from sustainability to the economic, social, and political empowerment of local people, but also because so many other development strategies have failed. Due to persistent economic crises and the difficulty of development via agricultural export economies, states have increasingly turned to nontraditional development strategies in order to boost foreign exchange earnings and as a means to minimize their exposure to international economic volatility. Due its ability to generate foreign exchange, ecotourism is "appealing to a vast range of interested groups because it simultaneously tries to satisfy and speak to numerous agendas: capitalist development, community development, poverty alleviation, wildlife conservation and environmental protection."[30] For instance the United Nations Environmental Programme (UNEP) found that "tourism's potential for creating employment, supporting livelihoods, and enabling sustainable development is huge, given that it is one of the main sources of foreign-exchange income."[31] Since agricultural export-led development has typically been very unstable, and industrial-led development has been difficult to attain, the range of development strategies for many poor countries have often been very limited. In addition, a strong reliance on agricultural exports has had a number of negative effects on the natural environment, both on the large-scale agro-export level which requires heavier use of chemicals as well as on the subsistence farming level, which often utilizes unsustainable techniques.

The growth of tourism in general and ecotourism in particular has created a unique opportunity for states to embark upon a development plan that employs ecotourism. The main focus of this book is to examine the way in which ecotourism fits in with more traditional development strategies. Ecotourism not only represents a potentially important source of foreign exchange, but can also serve as an intermediate step between an economy based on a small number of traditional agricultural exports and one that is made up of multiple streams of foreign exchange, including manufacturing. Ecotourism represents an intermediate step between agriculture and manufacturing-centered development because it can assist in phasing out agriculture by providing employment for those who previously made a living through farming and by providing a domestic market for food products. It can also assist in industrialization through establishing a number of conditions that help to increase investment in a country. Most importantly, it will do so with very important ecological constraints on incoming businesses. Another primary focus of this book is to examine the compatibility of ecotourism with foreign direct investment and the way in which policies that support ecotourism also support industrialization and foreign direct investment.

Ecotourism Success Story: Costa Rica

Costa Rica provides an excellent case study and model for countries that wish to utilize ecotourism as a development strategy, particularly in concert with attempts at industrialization via foreign direct investment. One of the things confronting a scholar studying Costa Rica is the almost mystical nature of the idea of Costa Rica exceptionalism on the one hand and the natural compulsion to be a skeptic on the other. Traveling in Costa Rica merely serves to further compound these two opposing ideals. Travelers leave Costa Rica thinking there must be *something* different about this place. Costa Rica stands out among the nations of Central America as a paragon of peace and stability and has long been seen as different from its neighbors by scholars as well as average Costa Ricans, many of whom will readily point out, *"Costa Rica es diferente"* and declare the differences they perceive between themselves and the rest of Central America. For decades, Costa Rican exceptionalism has served as the primary form of Costa Rican self-identity, reinforced by socialization. "Schools, the media, and popular tradition still inculcate Costa Ricans with the notion that their country stands apart from the rest of Central America's dictatorships, political violence, and underdevelopment."[32] Costa Rican history is replete with examples of similar external pressures acted upon differently in Costa Rica as compared to its neighbors, many of which have helped to create key differences between Costa Rica and the rest of Central America.

While the concept of Costa Rican exceptionalism and its veracity will be examined in detail in Chapter 2, it is important to note that the idea of Costa Rican exceptionalism permeates all corners of Costa Rican society and politics. While the accuracy of the idea of Costa Rican exceptionalism has its adherents as well as its detractors, one thing is certain; since the mid-twentieth century Costa Rica has enjoyed a peace and stability not present anywhere else in Central America and the Costa Rican economy has easily outpaced its neighbors.

Costa Rica has been able to parlay its peace and stability into concrete economic growth that has minimized the overall importance of and dependence on agricultural products as a percentage of economic activity. According to the World Bank, the GDP percentage of agricultural activities has fallen by about two-thirds since the early 1960s from 24.8 percent in the period 1961–1965 to 8.7 percent in the period 2001–2005.[33] Much of Costa Rica's move away from an agricultural-based economy was facilitated by its ability, starting in the 1980s, to harness its immense ecological gifts into a burgeoning ecotourism sector and, by the mid-1990s, had become a prime location for foreign direct investment.

The interplay of ecotourism and foreign direct investment is at the center of understanding how Costa Rica has developed over the past two decades. Due to Costa Rica's history and its unique natural resources, particularly with respect to biodiversity, Costa Rica has positioned itself as a prime destination for ecotourism as well as for foreign direct investment. Costa Rica has also been a world leader in conservation, a distinction that exceeds its geographical magnitude. Even with the differences between Costa Rica and its neighbors, it is possible for Costa Rica to serve as a model for the region because throughout its history it has had to deal with many of the same forces that have played a large role in determining the historical trajectory of its neighbors, but has dealt with them in a different way.

Organization of the Book

Chapter 1, "Ecotourism as a Development Strategy," examines the literature pertaining to ecotourism and the reasons why it can serve as an engine for development. With the increase in environmental awareness over the last couple decades, agriculture and environmentalism have often been at odds, primarily due to the heavy use of chemicals and other unsustainable methods in agriculture. This chapter also looks at volatility and other problems related to the agricultural-export market before looking at solutions to these problems in a development model that includes ecotourism. Ecotourism's major strengths include its ability to create jobs and entrepreneurship along with its focus on sustainability as well as the policy areas in which it deals with foreign direct investment. Due to the similarities between ecotourism and foreign direct investment, it is argued that they intersect in five important ways: issues of regime type and the rule of law, human capital development, proximity to the U.S. market and infrastructure issues, economic liberalization, and environmental protection.

Chapter 2, "Politics, Economics and Exceptionalism in Costa Rica," discusses the historical development of Costa Rica by focusing on the differences between Costa Rica and its neighbors. Beginning in the colonial period, there are a number of factors that differentiate Costa Rican history from the larger regional context. Scholars have long debated the effect of the colonial period on Costa Rican politics, especially the veracity of the rural democracy thesis. The rural democracy thesis argues that Costa Rican exceptionalism and later adherence to democracy and non-violence is due in large part to a number of factors that have their origins in the colonial period. These factors include a colonial Costa Rica that was heavily rural and agrarian, democratic very early on, racially homogenous due to the lack of a large indigenous population, and poverty stricken. Accordingly, colonial Costa Rica existed in an atmosphere of egalitarianism with little economic differentiation between various segments of society. An examination of the rural democracy thesis is the lens through which the development of later Costa Rican political economy is viewed, including the impact of coffee production on Costa Rican society, the crises of the 1930s and 1980s as well as the growth of neoliberalism in the 1990s and its effect on the development of ecotourism and high-tech manufacturing.

Chapter 3, "Ecotourism in Costa Rica," examines the development of eco-tourism in Costa Rican history. The combination of the economic crisis of the 1980s and rapid deforestation are integral to understanding the development of Costa Rican ecotourism because of the need for Costa Rica to diversify its exports. The diversification of exports was accomplished through the encouragement of nontraditional exports, in particular high value–added manufacturing and eco-tourism. Ecotourism also helped to reverse the trend of deforestation as land was set aside to be used for ecotourism. Much of the land that was set aside was incorporated into the Costa Rican national park system, which became the backbone of the ecotourism industry. This chapter also examines the role of the Instituto Costarricense de Turismo, whose job it is to manage ecotourism in Costa Rica.

Chapter 4, "Ecotourism, Foreign Direct Investment and the Costa Rican Model," develops the parameters of the Costa Rican model of development and investigates the intersection of ecotourism and foreign direct investment. At the heart of the Costa Rican model is the self-reinforcing nature of the policy concerns of both ecotourism and foreign direct investment due to the number of junctures in which development policy pertaining to ecotourism and foreign direct investment overlap. These five intersecting policy areas are: concerns of regime type and the rule of law, the development of human capital, policies that enhance Costa Rica's proximity to the United States and the country's infrastructure, economic liberalization and how ecotourism can serve as a check on the power of manufacturing due to the income generated by ecotourism, an activity that profits by preserving rather than destroying the natural environment.

Chapter 5, "Conclusion: Lessons from Costa Rica," first discusses the applicability of Costa Rica as a model for Central America and the status of ecotourism as a comparative advantage. From there, the chapter takes the lessons learned from the Costa Rican experience and crafts a set of policy recommendations for states to implement that support the development of ecotourism and foreign direct investment. One of the first steps is to formulate a plan that includes the long-range preservation of the environment upon which an ecotourism trade may be built. The chapter concludes by discussing policies that will support the development of both ecotourism and foreign direct investment.

Notes

1. Oscar Arias, "Peace, Development, and the Environment: Challenges to the Costa Rican Model." (Barnard Environmental lecture, American Association for the Advancement of Science, Washington, D.C., September 7, 2004).

2. Seema Bhatt and Syed Liyakhat, *Ecotourism Development in India: Communities, Capital and Conservation,* (New Delhi: Cambridge University Press India Pvt. Ltd., 2008), 10.

3. United Nations Environmental Programme. "Towards a Green Economy: Pathways to Sustainable Development and Poverty Eradication," accessed January 5, 2012, http://www.unep.org/greeneconomy.

4. Sterling Evans, *The Green Republic: A Conservation History of Costa Rica.* (Austin: University of Texas Press, 1999), 2.

5. Catherine Eade. "Costa Rica? The perfect destination for adventure seekers, wildlife fans and lovers of rolling green hills—'pura vida' indeed" *Daily Mail (UK)* January 6, 2011. http://www.dailymail.co.uk/travel/article-1341888/Costa-Rica-holidays-The-perfect-destination-adventure-seekers-wildlife-fans.html#ixzz1PAbqcA1X.

6.   David John Frank, Ann Hironaka and Evan Schofer, "The Nation-State and the Natural Environment over the Twentieth Century," *American Sociological Review* 65 (2000).

7.   David John Frank, "Science, Nature, and the Globalization of the Environment 1870-1990," *Social Forces* 76 (1997).

8.   Rebecca Maria Torres, "Gringolandia: The Construction of Tourist Space in Mexico," *Tourism Geographies* 4 (2005): 314.

9.   Bhatt and Liyakhat, *Ecotourism Development in India: Communities, Capital and Conservation.*

10.   Martha Honey, *Ecotourism and Sustainable Development: Who Owns Paradise?* Second Edition. (Washington, D.C., Island Press, 2008), 12-13.

11.   Ibid., 68.

12.   "What Is Ecotourism?" *International Ecotourism Society,* accessed October 27, 2011, http://www.ecotourism.org/what-is-ecotourism.

13.   Honey, *Ecotourism and Sustainable Development: Who Owns Paradise?* Second Edition, 29-31.

14.   Ibid., 32-33

15.   Geoffrey Wall and Alistair Mathieson, *Tourism: Change, Impacts and Opportunities.* (Harlow: Pearson Education Limited, 2006), 28.

16.   Donald V. L. MacLeod, "Tourism and the Globalization of a Canary Island," *The Journal of the Royal Anthropological Institute* 5 (1999): 453.

17.   Jennifer Kim Lian Chan and Tom Braun, "Ecotourists' Perception of Ecotourism Experience in Kinabatangan, Sabah, Malaysia," *Journal of Sustainable Tourism* 15 (2007): 586.

18.   Christos Zografos and David Allcroft, "The Environmental Values of Potential Ecotourists: A Segmentation Study," *Journal of Sustainable Tourism* 15 (2007): 59.

19.   Megan Epler Wood, "Ecotourism: Principles, Practices & Policies for Sustainability," (Paris: United Nations Environmental Program, 2002), 22.

20.   Laura Zanotti and Janet Chernola, "Conflicting Cultures of Nature: Ecotourism, Education and the Kayapo of the Brazilian Amazon," *Tourism Geographies* 10 (2008): 497.

21.   Auden Schendler, "Applying the Principles of Industrial Ecology to the Guest-Services Sector," *Journal of Industrial Ecology* 7 (2003): 135.

22.   Hector Ceballos-Lascurain, "The Future of Ecotourism," *Mexico Journal* 1 (1987).

23.   Caroline J. Stem, James P. Lassoie, David R. Lee and John W. Schelhas, "Community Participation in Ecotourism Benefits: The Link to Conservation Practices and Perspectives," *Society and Natural Resources* 16 (2003).

24.   Joan Giannecchini, "Ecotourism: New Partners, New Relationships," *Conservation Biology* 7 (1993): 431.

25.   Mark B. Orams, "The Effectiveness of Environmental Education: Can we turn the Tourists into 'Greenies?'" *Progress in Tourism and Hospitality Research* (1997): 304.

26.   Sheila Peake, Peter Innes and Pam Dyer, "Ecotourism and Conservation: Factors influencing effective conservation messages," *Journal of Sustainable Tourism* 17 (2009).

27.   Julian Clifton and Angela Benson, "Planning for Sustainable Tourism: The Case for Research Ecotourism in Developing Country Destinations," *Journal of Sustainable Tourism* 14 (2006): 241.

28.   Kathleen L. Andereck, "Tourists' perceptions of environmentally responsible innovation at tourism businesses," *Journal of Sustainable Tourism* 17 (2009).

29. Stuart Cotrell, Rene van der Ruim, Patricia Ankersmid and Liesbeth Kelder, "Measuring the Sustainability of Tourism in Manuel Antonio and Texel: A Tourist Perspective," *Journal of Sustainable Tourism* 12 (2004): 427.

30. Rosaleen Duffy, "Neoliberalising Nature: Global Networks and Ecotourism Development in Madagascar," *Journal of Sustainable Tourism* 16 (2008): 341.

31. United Nations Environmental Programme, "Towards a Green Economy: Pathways to Sustainable Development and Poverty Eradication.

32. John A. Booth, Christine J, Wade and Thomas W. Walker, *Understanding Central America: Global Forces, Rebellion, and Change.* (Boulder: Westview Press, 2006), 53.

33. World Bank, "Costa Rica Country Economic Memorandum: The Challenges for Sustained Growth," (Poverty Reduction and Economic Management Sector Unit Report #36180-CR, September 20, 2006).

Chapter 1
Ecotourism as a
Development Strategy

One promising source of foreign exchange for poor countries is the pursuit of ecotourism as a development strategy. While development strategies based on mass tourism have been encouraged by multilateral lending and aid institutions for several decades, ecotourism provides a unique set of attributes such as a focus on sustainability and empowerment of local people that shows exceptional promise for more broad-based development. In a study by Weinberg, Bellows, and Ekster, they found that "ecotourism has brought varied positive changes, including more jobs and income leading to an improved standard of living; better and more varied services; a conservationist ethic; better training; the start of recycling; and a bilingual population."[1] Ecotourism works particularly well when paired with policies that attract foreign direct investment due to the number of policy areas in which the two intersect. These points of intersection provide unique insights into how an ecotourism and foreign direct investment model for economic development could be formulated. This chapter will discuss the ways in which a development model based upon ecotourism coupled with the pursuit of foreign direct investment provides a new path toward economic development.

Agricultural Exports, Conservation and Ecotourism

One of the primary reasons export agriculture has been unsuccessful in providing long-term economic growth is the inherent terms of trade problems between the developed world, which tends to export manufactured goods, and the developing world, which tends to export agricultural products. Export-led agricultural development has been difficult due in large part to the ever-increasing price of manufactured goods as well as commodities such as oil and the ever-decreasing

13

value of agricultural goods. As a result, poor countries are paying a larger and larger share of their income just to maintain the same standard of living, making economic expansion very difficult. Development through agricultural export is also very challenging due to the inherent volatility of the commodities market coupled with most poor countries' focus on relatively few products for export, which helps to exacerbate the effect of even small downward movements in the market.

Not only have agricultural export–driven economies had limited success in producing widespread wealth within the developing world, but a burgeoning environmental movement around the globe has placed agricultural production, with its heavy use of chemicals and the proliferation of unsustainable practices, at odds with environmental conservation. These problems are particularly acute in the developing world because of the number of countries that rely on large-scale agricultural production as the main source of foreign exchange. The environmental damage caused by agriculture puts it directly in conflict with attempts to promote ecotourism because of ecotourism's inherent necessity to conserve the natural environment.

An orientation toward sustainability affects both state behavior, particularly with respect to environmental laws and regulations, and the individual's orientation toward the environment. Since both states and individuals have come to redefine their relationship to the natural world, increases in environmental regulations, laws, and treaties often take aim at unsustainable and destructive agricultural practices, which increase tensions between agricultural interests and environmentalists. Given these tensions, Geldermann and Kogel argue that "the most difficult global task will be to produce large amounts of good quality food by protecting the environment. Economy and ecology seem to be on opposite sides of this dilemma."[2]

Not only is it difficult to have large-scale agricultural production within the confines of environmental sustainability, industrial agriculture focused on the international export market:

> seems least likely to benefit from new environmental laws. In many countries, agriculture is not capital intensive and has a very low profit margin. Moreover, many international environmental treaties and organizations specifically curtail agriculture by placing limits on deforestation, fisheries and so on. While it is common to assume that environmentalism targets industry, the agricultural sector may be affected more significantly.[3]

Longo and York found a positive link between export-focused agriculture and the consumption of fertilizer, pesticide, energy and the use of capital intensive practices in agriculture and the growing global trade in agricultural commodities.[4] Modern farming techniques, particularly the use of chemical fertilizers and pesticides, are employed to increase yields by using an ever-increasing amount of chemicals on ever smaller plots of land, thus increasing the concentration of chemicals. For instance, since 1950 crop yields in the United States have increased by 100 percent on 25 percent less land, while India has seen a nearly four-fold increase in wheat production with only a 60 percent increase in farmland.[5] Improvements in agricultural technology play a large role in agricultural intensification because it "produces larger market benefits on higher-quality land. Thus, all actors involved in agricultural production and marketing tend to concentrate their resources on the best land available to them, and they intensify their efforts in terms of frequency of use, labor, and capital investment."[6]

One of the best ways for government policy to begin resolving the conflict between agriculture and environmental conservation is to set aside environmentally sensitive areas as national parks, making them off-limits for agricultural production. The formation of a national park system has been especially successful in Costa Rica and serves as the backbone of the ecotourism industry. For many who engage in subsistence farming, the formation of national parks is not always welcome, and government policy regarding seizure of land for national parks has not always been just. Rutagarama and Martin found that much of the problem stems from the fact that "the idea of national parks is a predominantly Western one rooted in a way of valuing natural assets that diverges from that of resource dependent people."[7] Due to differences between conservationists and those who engage in subsistence agriculture, the problem of balancing people's livelihoods and environmental protection is very difficult to solve since agriculture and environmentalism are too often mutually exclusive. Not only do a large percentage of people in the developing world depend on small-scale farming for survival, many continue to use premodern agricultural techniques, which often cause soil erosion, water depletion, pollution, deforestation, depletion of fisheries, and habitat disruption or depletion. Ecotourism holds the potential to complement environmental protection and to provide employment for those displaced from agriculture, but it must empower and include local people in decision-making processes and share the wealth among stakeholders. Not surprisingly Ormsby and Mannle in a study of National Parks in Madagascar found that "residents interviewed who were recipients of benefits from the park, such as income from ecotourism, legal resource use, or direct recipients of park-funded development projects, had positive attitudes towards the park."[8]

Within the context of declining terms of trade and loss of income from agriculture, one of the most important things ecotourism can do is to create backward linkages within an economy, particularly by using locally grown food that would otherwise be exported. Doing so is beneficial not only because it would help to shift agricultural goods away from the international market for use in domestic markets, but it would also save money. Diverting agricultural products to the domestic market would have a positive effect on the larger economy because "developing backward linkages to local agriculture is critical in reducing foreign exchange leakages and increasing local multiplier effects."[9]

The use of local food for ecotourists not only helps farmers recoup potential revenue lost from environmental regulations, but also adds to the allure of the destination. Ecotourists, who tend to be more adventurous than most mainstream tourists, will help the local food market because of their desire for local cuisine, which is often an attitudinal extension of their overall desire for the exotic and unique. Torres found that "tourists on the less institutionalized and more adventurous side of the continuum display a stronger interest in trying local foods and have less desire for home country cuisine."[10] The combination of the desire to travel somewhere "off the beaten path" coupled with the affordability of traveling to the developing world has acted as a catalyst for the growth of ecotourism. Even in a poor economic climate, the Caribbean Tourism Organization found that customers have a willingness to travel further afield and are now choosing Central America, China, and Asia and are increasingly demanding a "unique experience" as they wish to be distinguished from those who pay for a luxury vacation.[11]

What Can Ecotourism Contribute to Economic Development?

Due to the myriad economic crises over the last several decades, many countries in the developing world have been forced to embark upon a plan of structural adjustment in an attempt to lower their debt burden. These plans are often centered on an export-driven model of development and the need to diversify and expand their agricultural-export portfolios to create additional sources of foreign exchange. Another common strategy is the development of a tourism industry, particularly among tropical countries whose climates are suitable for mass tourism. Particularly attractive to some multilateral institutions is ecotourism due to its focus on sustainability and possible further diversification of a country's foreign exchange, thus creating long-term economic development. Consequently, ecotourism "has been promoted by a range of organizations including the United Nations, the World Bank, national governments and environmental NGOs as a means of achieving sustainable development."[12]

Due to the similarities between the tourist's and investor's desire for a location, tourism requires the sort of neoliberal economic policies normally associated with foreign direct investment. As Tamborini points out, growth in tourism can be attributed to "the tourism industry's affinity with neoliberal policy reforms which emphasize global integration and outward looking development."[13] In many ways, tourism and the free movement of people around the globe exemplifies economic liberalism and is illustrative of the forces of globalization. MacLeod argues that "tourism is the epitome of global flows, the free (or unforced) movement of people around the globe, carriers of cultural capital, users of technological networks, transmitters of cross-cultural ideas; in fact the tourist personifies globalization."[14]

Wall and Mathieson give six important economic benefits of tourism as an engine of economic development by contributing to:

1. Foreign exchange earnings and the balance of payments;
2. The generation of income;
3. The generation of employment;
4. The improvement of economic structures;
5. The encouragement of entrepreneurial activity;

6.   The stimulation of regional economies and the mitigation of regional economic disparities.[15]

As generators of income, ecotourism and export industries share many goals. Thus policies that support one inherently support the other with government playing an important role in formulating policy in a way that benefits multiple businesses across both industries. In developing countries in particular, government incentives play an important part in the pace of economic growth and can often make an important difference. In Costa Rica, for example, there was an extensive construction boom in the early 1990s when the government offered tax breaks to tourism industries similar to those offered to the export industry.[16] These policies encouraged the desired investment across both tourism and export industry and provided an important macroeconomic benefit.

Ecotourism also contributes to economic development by helping countries move away from economies based on agricultural export dependence and its inherent problems of volatility. The volatility of agricultural exports represents a significant impediment to economic expansion, and the problem is further exacerbated by the fact that the causes of volatility are largely out of their control. These factors include "the falling value of the US dollar, commodity futures speculation, and trade measures."[17] In addition to international economic factors, volatility in agricultural markets is further out of the hands of producers because of variations in supply caused by either favorable or unfavorable natural conditions during a growing season, which have sharp influences on price. The combination of market volatility and natural conditions makes farming in the developing world a very difficult proposition, particularly for small-scale farmers. "Small scale farmers must contend not only with the uncertainties of Mother Nature and the boom-and-bust cycles in commodity prices but also with limited economic resources and political power; they are typically at a disadvantage in global markets and often receive relatively low prices for their products."[18]

Another common strategy to boost the commodities trade among agricultural-export countries is the focus on a narrow band of high-value products in an attempt to boost foreign exchange earnings. Oftentimes when states rely on a small number of agricultural exports and try to diversify by selecting a high value product, they still fall victim to volatility and unstable market conditions. Multilateral institutions often contribute to this problem by encouraging many different countries to specialize in only a few products. One example of this problem is the encouragement by many multilateral lending and aid organizations for the development of a coffee-growing industry to boost foreign exchange. The widespread adoption of this plan, coupled with the effect its adoption has on boom and boost cycles, makes the coffee export market exceedingly volatile and inhibits the profitability for small growers who face many challenges with profitability.

Since the primary problem for states that rely on agricultural-export economies is the inherent volatility and subordinate position of the developing world in international markets, one of the best ways in which a state can minimize its international market risk is by using a development plan under which they have a greater amount of control. Ecotourism can provide a much more stable source of foreign exchange because it is less beholden to prices set by the international market. In states that utilize ecotourism, they can shield themselves from international market volatility because the prices for tourism are set domestically. Not only are states able to have much more control over prices, they can do so with much less competition, especially for countries that have a truly unique destination. For instance, while there are dozens of countries that sell coffee on the international market, there is only one Monteverde Cloud Forest. This gives Costa Rica much more discretion over the revenue generated through a variety of taxes and fees related to a visit. This also includes charging more for some destinations, something Costa Rica has done at its most popular national parks.[19]

The combination of a unique ecotourism destination coupled with the high market elasticity of tourism, means that small changes in the personal income of tourists amount to much larger receipts for a country's tourism industry. Dellaert and Linberg found that "there is the potential for greater price differentiation between tourists as well as for different pricing and promotion policies for travel products offered at different price levels. In particular, high income tourists can be expected to be less sensitive to average price changes as well as less consistent in their response to such changes."[20] The growth in ecotourism over the last several decades has proven that people are increasingly apt to spend larger and larger amounts of money on a truly unique trip. The ability for countries such as Costa Rica to provide a truly unique excursion for ecotourists is an important comparative advantage.

States that rely on revenue from ecotourism are also less likely to be affected by trade restrictions because their main source of income is derived from the movement of people in and out of the country. Conversely, international trade can often be hampered by the placement of trade restrictions such as tariffs, duties or some other political measure to limit a country's export capability. The sort of policies that would limit the exportation of a product out of a country and into another would almost never affect the tourism industry. With only very limited exceptions, there are no trade wars over tourism. With the predominance of tourists originating from the developed world, there is also little chance that advanced democracies would inhibit the movement of its people in and out of the country. "For the most part tourist destinations have free and repeat access to the international tourist market . . . tourist demand is largely governed by market forces and not government policy."[21] In the absence of government policy that would inhibit the flow of tourists, the biggest danger stems from issues of political and social stability and the reaction of tourists to spikes in violence in popular ecotourism destinations.

Another important contribution to economic development is the ability of ecotourism to create jobs and opportunities for entrepreneurship. Since the ecotourism industry is labor intensive, and the jobs are impossible to outsource or automate, it holds the potential to be an excellent source of employment, with some jobs paying more than traditional industries. For instance, in some locales a tour or dive guide can make more than double what he or she would earn in a traditional village industry.[22] While sometimes seasonal, ecotourism jobs also provide employment for a range of skill sets including jobs for low-skilled workers who might otherwise be difficult to employ. Many of these jobs are created in rural areas among groups that have high levels of unemployment.

The growth of ecotourism also provides excellent opportunities for the development of locally run businesses and is uniquely positioned to assist the development of locales that have long been ignored by attempts at industrial development often centered in urban areas. One of the most interesting ways that ecotourism has created employment opportunities in rural areas is the training of locals as naturalist guides. Often these programs can train farmers who have been displaced due to conservation efforts or even the training of former wildlife poachers into second careers as naturalist guides. Poachers in particular are an interesting case because their illicit activities provided them with unique knowledge of the location of unusual flora and fauna.

Ecotourism, especially when driven by a larger movement among states toward a more open economy, can contribute significantly to a state's level of entre-preneurship. Although it is common near ecotourism sites to encounter foreign owned businesses engaged in ecotourism-related commerce, ecotourism can provide a unique opportunity for entrepreneurship. "Many middle and lower-middle class Costa Ricans have managed to move into auxiliary businesses associated with ecotourism . . . on balance, ecotourism has brought more income to many Costa Ricans."[23] The growth of ecotourism provides much room for the expansion of businesses related to the tourist trade such as transportation companies, ecotourism guides, restaurants, and souvenir sellers, the vast majority of which would be started by entrepreneurs from the local population. In a study of reef tourism in Belize, Moreno found that "entrepreneurial industries have grown around tourism, including laundries, boat and spare room rentals, and internet cafes."[24] In order for this to happen, Hawkins found that it was necessary to have "strategic planning, financial analysis, and business plan development . . . to encourage a project pipeline necessary to create entrepreneurial-driven sustainable development designed to improve the quality and viability of ecotourism."[25] Not only can ecotourism help to create businesses in associated areas of the economy, it can also necessitate improvements in areas that may have spillover effects for other types of economic development. These include improvements in education, infrastructure quality, and economic policies favorable to economic development. Furthermore, Schofer and Grandados argue that new business opportunities outside of ecotourism exist based on environmental preservation and awareness due to the fact that the "global institutionalization of environmentalism may drive the growth of new industries, reduce comparative advantages of polluters and, over the long term, reconstruct economic value, generating benefits for pro-environmental countries."[26]

While ecotourism can provide increased economic development on the macro level, in order to truly adhere to its core values, it must help to create income among local populations. One of the biggest inhibitors for local economic growth via ecotourism is the problem of economic leakage. Estimates of the average leakage from tourism range from 40 to as high as 90 percent.[27] The greatest part of economic leakage occurs when portions of the trip are purchased within the ecotourist's home country such as airfare or payment to tour companies originating outside the destination country. In order to minimize the problems of economic leakage it is necessary to educate travelers to purchase as much of their trip at the destination as possible. This is facilitated by encouraging local entrepreneurship, which will also help to minimize the amount of income that is either spent in the ecotourist's home country before the trip, or sent out of the country to foreign owners. Since the emergence of the ecotourism industry, Costa Rica has been increasingly more successful in encouraging tourists to plan their trip while in country. In 2010, approximately one-quarter of arriving tourists planned their trip upon arrival.[28]

Tourist preferences for familiar food and products from home are also an important source of economic leakage since these products need to be imported. The problem of leakage due to the importation of food to satisfy tourist demand is particularly acute among large resorts because of "industry attempts to satisfy perceived tourist food preferences even if it results in a high import bill." (Torres 2002, 283)

Akama and Kieti give seven strategies for tourism to contribute to local community development:

1. Expansion of local employment and self-employment;
2. Expansion of informal sector opportunities;
3. Development of partnership amongst public and private sectors, NGOs and local communities;
4. Improving social and cultural impacts;
5. Increasing local access to infrastructure and services provided for tourists;
6. Increasing participation of local people in decision-making process;
7. Capacity-building to enable their participation.[29]

These seven principles seek to empower local communities and to retain as much income as possible. These efforts, however, will go unrealized if travelers are not educated in the social and economic ramifications of their spending on local populations and economies. The key to minimizing economic leakage is to empower local people to have control over their own future so that they can actively pursue entrepreneurial opportunities in ecotourism that keep the money local. One of the best ways to empower individuals and to encourage them to participate in the economy is through a legal and regulatory framework that is designed for this pur- pose. Any government policy that enhances an individual's ability to participate in the market will serve to empower that individual. One of the most important aspects of ecotourism is that it is intrinsically local and the vast majority of transactions associated with ecotourism can be purchased at the destination, as long as tourists are aware of their options. This inherently local setting for ecotourism is one of its strongest attributes.

Ecotourism and the Environment

One of the most important features of ecotourism is its ability to aid in the promotion of economic development and the empowerment of local people while doing so in a sustainable way. The merging of sustainability and economic development creates a balance between development and conservation, which can often be difficult to maintain. On one hand, ecotourism encourages conservation in the sense that fragile areas are protected from use and possible destruction by other parts of the economy. However, many ecotourism enthusiasts have become concerned that the rising number of tourists will strain the capacity of ecologically fragile areas and the long-term effects of that strain. For instance, Giannecchini points out that "conservationists must be concerned about the impact of the burgeoning numbers of visitors to the wilderness. These visitors represent the potential to generate revenue for the support of protected areas, as well as to destroy them through overuse and abuse."[30] Overcapacity can also strain an already overwhelmed infrastructure and cause other problems because in some countries with potential ecotourism destinations "sewerage, water, transportation, and solid waste disposal systems are inadequate to service the number of visitors."[31]

Ecotourism's mission can also be undermined by greenwashing (also referred to as ecotourism lite), which is the attempt to make a business or activity appear environmentally friendly when it is not. Due to the inherent fuzziness in the definitions of both sustainability and ecotourism in the minds of many people, it can often be very difficult to know exactly what a hotel or tour company implies by ecotourism, environmentally friendly, or sustainable. While some of what could be referred to as ecotourism lite is not malicious so much as simplistic, sometimes the deception is an intentional play on people's better motives and is often just mass tourism packaged to appear as if it is attentive to the environment and socially consciousness. "Ecotourism lite is propelled by travel agents, tour operators, airlines and cruise lines, large hotel and resort chains, and international tourism organizations, which promote quick, superficially 'green' visits within conventional packages."[32] Not only do these practices dilute the essential qualities of ecotourism, but they also fool customers into thinking they are acting in an environmentally and socially responsible way, when in fact they are not.

One of the best ways to ensure that ecotourism is done in a way consistent with its values is through the development of both national and international certification programs that assess long-term sustainability through a consistent set of criteria. Honey estimates the number of "green" tourism certification programs that serve as voluntary, third-party, multi-stakeholder programs and award logos based on environmental, economic and social criteria to be between 60 and 80.[33] The use of certification programs is an important step toward sustainable practices and moving ecotourism from a set of ideals to a set of definable practices. As very few of these programs are global in scope, it is also important that standards and practices be applied across individual countries so that ecotourism lives up to its ideals and benefits the local population.

To minimize the impact of ecotourism visitors on fragile environs, it is necessary for there to be sound management practices that actively administer the site to reduce the possibility of damage. Wall and Mathieson provide eight principles to minimize the adverse impact of tourists:

1.   Concentrate or channel visitors and their vehicles into places where they can be managed;
2.   Attract people away from vulnerable areas;
3.   Disperse use over a wide area so no part is unacceptably altered;
4.   Institute a system of rotation so that used areas get a chance to recuperate;
5.   Use hard surfaces, barriers and specialized site layouts and designs to control use;
6.   Employ cultural treatments including watering, fertilizing, seeding of durable species and artificial loosening of compact soils;
7.   Pricing;
8.   Information provision through such means as signage and interpretation.[34]

These principles are useful because they require very little investment and mostly speak to the ability of park management to control crowds and to reduce damage to the park. The major investment in park management is the training of park rangers, which can be very difficult for poor countries due to lack of funding. Lack of funding can also affect the management of ecologically fragile areas because too often the enforcement of environmental regulations is constrained by the lack of state institutional capacity. An excellent way to solve both the problems of management and lack of institutional capacity is through citizen involvement in environmental non-government organizations (NGOs). NGOs not only boost citizen involvement and empowerment, but also can assist the state when necessary. Former Director of the Costa Rican National Parks Department Mario Boza argues that citizen involvement is the key to ensuring long-term sustainability:

> Conservation is a heavy burden for the government of a developing country. This is why the population needs to be actively involved through organized NGOs, such as associations, foundations, or clubs. These NGOs can play an active role in raising international funds, helping with protection, and developing environ-mental education programs.[35]

Using ecotourism as a sustainable economic development strategy requires that government and the private sector take the long view on development and not seek out money that can be made from exploiting natural resources in the short term. For too many developing countries the temptation to take the quick money, or the lack of institutional capacity to formulate and carry out a long-term plan, hampers their ability to utilize ecotourism. For instance, governments may decide to allow logging in old growth forest because they can get a great deal of badly needed funds more quickly than waiting for slower and more sustainable strategies.

Ecotourism also serves to empower environmental preservation because it places value on natural assets. By commoditizing natural resources, ecotourism is able to provide a clear development strategy rooted in economic terms. The economic value of natural assets gives power to the ecotourism industry because so many people make their living from ecotourism, which aims to profit from what it preserves, that the ecotourism industry can have a strong voice in policy matters. Due to the nature of ecotourism "avoiding loss of ecosystems by conservation, particularly of forests, mangroves, wetlands, and the coastal zone, including coral reefs, is a sound investment from a cost-benefit analysis. This appears to hold from both a societal investment perspective as well as a private one."[36]

While poor countries may be tempted to take the "quick cash," Honey found that many ecotourism ventures are more profitable than the revenue generated from more destructive activities. For instance, a study in South Africa found that net income from wildlife tourism was almost eleven times more than from cattle ranching while the job creation capacity was fifteen times greater. Other studies have valued a lion in Kenya at $7,000 per year and a herd of elephants at $610,000 a year in terms of tourism proceeds. A 2001 study of the Turks and Caicos islands found that a spiny lobster was more valuable in the water for ecotourists than on a dinner plate.[37] Examples such as these involve a great deal of long-term planning and a government and people who are dedicated to environmental sustainability. At the beginning of the ecotourism boom in the late 1980s, Guillermo Canessa, former head of wildlife conservation for the Costa Rican government, summed up the challenges of convincing poor farmers not to cut down trees because it is not in their long-term economic interest "the tourist industry can offer an alternative for them. We can demonstrate that the trees can be worth more to them standing than felled."[38] It is often very difficult to convince people that they can profit through the non-use of the environment, yet when axes are replaced by cameras and ecotourism is established, the argument becomes much more convincing. Since many natural features represent finite resources, their preservation is beneficial to human needs in the long run. While ecotourism utilizes the natural environment it does not *use* it by depleting finite resources. Not only can environmental preservation act as the crux of the moneymaking potential of the ecotourism industry and inform a country's environmental policies, it can also contribute to preservation of the natural environment in other ways:

> The dependence of tourism on the quality of the natural environment also places it in a special position in terms of environmental sustainability. The (Travel and Tourism) industry can make a positive contribution to the quality of the natural environment by, for example, communicating the value of the natural environment to residents, by creating business incentives for environmental improvements, and through raising awareness of environmental issues and encouraging environmental conservation.[39]

Ecotourism also represents an opportunity for sustainable development because it utilizes already existing features of the natural environment such as native rain forests, wildlife, and other ecological gifts to foster development. Development therefore becomes based upon the locale in and of itself without the need for large-scale development as would be necessary for development based solely upon manufacturing. This improves the sustainability of ecotourism and also helps to get local people involved in the industry since they would be the most likely to benefit from the expansion of visitors. As Binns and Nel point out, this has led to development in many areas that were once marginalized:

> The identification of localities as a result of their location, natural attractions, and tourist related facilities, has enabled once marginalized areas, such as Mediterranean and Caribbean islands to enjoy new-found economic prosperity.[40]

The Intersection of Foreign Direct Investment and Ecotourism

Once ecotourism is established, it can play a central role in economic development because of the similarities between the needs of ecotourism and industrial economic policy. If ecotourism and its critical focus on environmental preservation precede industrialization, a country is much more likely to industrialize with a stronger set of environmental laws and regulations enacted by those who earn their living by preserving the environment. Due to the relative ease of ecotourism development versus industrial development, many states would be well served to begin with policies that encourage ecotourism development first, thus creating an atmosphere in which foreign direct investment becomes more likely. These intersections of ecotourism development and foreign direct investment include issues of regime type and the rule of law, human capital development, proximity to the U.S. market and infrastructure issues, economic liberalization, and environmental protection.

The popular perception of foreign direct investment is that companies' offshore operations primarily save money on labor costs. Although labor costs play a role in a company's decision-making process when locating operations outside the country, there are many factors that inform decisions such as location, the skill of the workforce and the political climate of the country. Furthermore, there may be many hidden costs to foreign direct investment such as "vendor search cost, travel transition cost, layoffs and ongoing costs of managing the contract"[41] so the decision to make a large investment in a country is made for a variety of reasons. Therefore, when looking to expand abroad, companies look at the entire package a country has to offer and seek out a destination that has the most attractive set of attributes. Similarly, tourists seek to maximize the positive aspects in the choice of destination and rarely take trips based on a single factor. Tripathi and Siddiqui found that the most important tourist preference is value for the money, followed by security, information, with relatively less importance placed on variety of sight-seeing options, complaint redress and modes of access.[42]

In this way it is possible to begin conceptualizing foreign direct investment and tourism as similar activities, with each making an important investment based on a number of factors in pursuit of value. For an effective strategy built upon ecotourism and foreign direct investment, it is necessary for a country to create policies that reinforce their ability to attract both investment and tourists. If a vacationing tourist is viewed in terms of making an investment, the intersection between policies that encourage tourism and foreign direct investment becomes clearer.

First, both ecotourism and foreign direct investment are concerned with regime type and the rule of law and thus desire a location that has experienced long-term political and social stability and values that flow from such stability. The extent to which a locale is an attractive investment of an ecotourist's time and vacation money or as a destination for foreign direct investment greatly influences the selection processes of both. In particular, tourists and foreign companies want to invest in a place that can ensure a high level of personal safety. The rule of law is also important because lawlessness can easily keep tourists and foreign companies away. Tourists are particularly sensitive to personal safety issues and will stay away from countries that have consistent, problems of violence and lawlessness as the large drop in tourism to Mexico over the last couple years has shown. In order to assist in the creation of social and political stability, it is important for government policy to focus on policing and on the institutional capacity of its court system.

The second policy intersection deals with the need to build human capital. Countries that are better able to build human capital are much more likely to attract tourists and foreign companies with a focus on building an educated and skilled workforce. Both tourists and companies looking to invest are more likely to select a location in which the population is better educated and has the skills needed to provide the work or service desired. Ecotourists in particular also desire a high level of expertise for naturalist guides in order to make the trip more well rounded and fulfilling by adding to the educational element. The education and expertise of naturalist guides also serve to accentuate the value of a destination because they can help an ecotourist to better understand what they are seeing and thus better appreciate it. While instruction in technology or English is best suited to formal education, this is not necessarily the case for ecotourism. Many of the very best naturalist guides someone may encounter do not have a formal education in ecology or environmental science, but instead have built a lifetime of knowledge based on their inherent interest in the local environment.

The third intersection deals with proximity and infrastructure. Obviously a country is bound to its geography; however, there are ways in which infrastructure can enhance its proximity to the source of ecotourists and foreign direct investment, and the goals of both ecotourism and foreign direct investment are very closely related with regard to infrastructure. Both ecotourism and FDI want to get in and out of the country with relative ease, most likely through a modern airport. Each entity also wants to be able to move its products within the country via a workable transportation system. Given the extraordinary difficulty of infrastructure projects for poor countries, it is extremely important that initial projects are targeted toward clear objectives and sources of income.

The fourth intersection is the desire for economic liberalization measures and integration into the global economy. The desire of businesses to build a facility in a place that makes economic transactions simple is easy to understand. Interestingly, the desire of tourists and businesses closely intersect with respect to economic liberalization. Both want to go to a location that is integrated into the world economy and can provide all the modern economic conveniences, most especially easy access to their money. Economic liberalization also overlaps with concerns about the rule of law because of the fear of economic expropriation by the government. Not only does allaying fears of economic expropriation provide stability to the economy, but also companies that do not fear expropriation by the government will be much more likely to reinvest. Since economic liberalization overlaps with concerns over the rule of law, the pursuit of enhancements to the institutional capacity of the judicial system will also help to mitigate fears of tourists and investors. Furthermore, government policy should work to create a regulatory environment that encourages business growth and expansion, but does so within the context of the values of ecotourism.

The fifth intersection, environmental protection, is not as direct as the other four because ecotourism has a constraining rather than a complementary effect on industry. One of the strongest attributes of ecotourism is its ability to constrain environmentally destructive practices by industry. Since ecotourism revenue is predicated on preservation of the environment, it is important for the ecotourism industry to have a voice. The best way to do this is through an acknowledgment that long-term preservation is more profitable than exploitation. This will allow ecotourism to have a strong voice because of its important role in the national economy as a major source of income and thus its requirements need to be adhered to for it to continue contributing to the national economy. If policy is formulated in such a way that ecotourism acts as a path to industrialization, it will already be an important player in the economy and voice for conservation. Ecotourism and policy-based restraints on industrial pollution will help to attract high-tech manufacturing and other low environmental impact manufacturing, as has been the case in Costa Rica.

Due to the policy areas in which ecotourism and foreign direct investment intersect, governments should consider building a plan of ecotourism development leading to industrialization. Each desires a location that is politically, socially and economically stable, possesses high levels of human capital, a working infrastructure, and is integrated into the world's economy. Furthermore, when ecotourism precedes foreign direct investment and industrialization, there will be important constraints on the environmental behavior of manufacturers. Chapter 4 will broaden the discussion of these intersections including the ways in which each policy area has intersected in the development of Costa Rica. The manner in which Costa Rica has managed these five intersections can act as a guide for other countries that want to utilize the combination of ecotourism and foreign direct investment as a development strategy.

Notes

1. Adam Weinberg, Story Bellows and Dara Ekster, "Sustaining Ecotourism: Insights and Implications from Two Successful Case Studies," *Society and Natural Resources* 15 (2002): 374.

2. U. Geldermann and K-H Kogel, "Nature's Concept. The 'New Agriculture' amidst Ecology, Economy, and the Demythologization of the Gene," *Journal of Agronomy and Crop Science 188* (2002): 368.

3. Evan Schofer and Francisco J. Granados, "Environmentalism Globalization and National Economies 1980-2000," *Social Forces* 85 (1980), 968.

4. Stefano Longo and Richard York, "Agricultural Exports and the Environment: A Cross National Study of Fertilizer and Pesticide Consumption," *Rural Sociology* 73 (2008).

5. Robert Paarlberg, "The Ethics of Modern Agriculture," *Society* 46 (2009):7.

6. Luis García-Barrios, Yankuic M Galván-Miyoshi, Ingrid Abril Valdivieso-Pérez, Omar R Masera, Gerardo Bocco and John Vandermeer, "Neotropical Forest Conservation, Agricultural Intensification, and Rural Out-migration: The Mexican Experience," *BioScience* 29 (2009): 864.

7. Eugene Rutagarama and Adrian Smith, "Partnerships for Protected Area Conservation in Rwanda," *The Geographical Journal* 172 (2006): 303.

8. Alison Ormsby and Kathryn Mannle, "Ecotourism Benefits and the Role of Local Guided at Masoala National Park, Madagascar," *Journal of Sustainable Tourism* 14 (2006): 284.

9. Rebecca Torres, "Toward a better understanding of tourism and agricultural linkages in the Yucatan; Tourist food consumption and preferences," *Tourism Geographies* 4 (2002): 283.

10. Ibid., 285.

11. Caribbean Tourism Organization, "A Rough Ride for Luxury Travel, Accessed October 10, 2010, http://www.onecaribbean.org/content/files/PwCRoughRide4luxury travel Dec08.pdf.

12. Rosaleen Duffy, "Neoliberalising Nature: Global Networks and Ecotourism Development in Madagascar," *Journal of Sustainable Tourism 16* (2008): 330.

13. Christopher R. Tamborini, "Work, Wages and Gender in Export-Oriented Cities: Global Assembly Versus International Tourism in Mexico," *Bulletin of Latin America Research* 26 (2007): 30.

14. Donald V. L. MacLeod, "Tourism and the Globalization of a Canary Island," *The Journal of the Royal Anthropological Institute 5* (1999): 445-446.

15. Geoffrey Wall and Alistair Mathieson, *Tourism: Change, Impacts and Opportunities.* (Harlow, Pearson Education Limited, 2006), 89.

16. Mary A. Clark, "Nontraditional Export Promotion in Costa Rica: Sustaining Export-Led Growth," *Journal of Interamerican Studies and World Affairs* 37 (1995): 211.

17. Jennifer Clapp, "Food Price Volatility in the Global South: Considering the Global Economic Context," *Third World Quarterly* 30 (2009): 1194.

18. Deborah Sick, "Coffee, Farming Families, and Fair Trade in Costa Rica," *Latin American Research Review* 43 (2008): 193-194.

19. Lisa C. Chase, David R. Lee, William D. Schulze and Deborah J. Anderson, "Ecotourism Demand and Differential Pricing of National Park Access in Costa Rica," *Land Economics* 74 (1998): 480.

20. Benedict G. C. Dellaert and Kreg Lindberg, "Variation in Tourist Price Sensitivity: A Stated Preference Model to Capture the Joint Impact of Differences in Systematic Utility and Response Consistency," *Leisure Sciences* 25 (2003): 94.

21. Geoffrey Wall and Alistair Mathieson, *Tourism: Change, Impacts and Opportunities.* (Harlow: Pearson Education Limited, 2006), 84.

22. Peter S. Moreno, "Ecotourism Along the Meso-American Caribbean Reef: The Impacts of Foreign Investment," *Human Ecology* 33 (2005): 229.

23. Martha Honey, "Giving a Grade to Costa Rica's Green Tourism," *NACLA Report on the Americas* XXXVI (2003): 44-45.

24. Moreno, "Ecotourism Along the Meso-American Caribbean Reef: The Impacts of Foreign Investment," 229.

25. Donald E. Hawkins, "A Protected Areas Ecotourism Competitive Cluster Approach to Catalyse Biodiversity Conservation and Economic Growth in Bulgaria," *Journal of Sustainable Tourism* 12 (2005): 241.

26. Schofer and Granados, "Environmentalism Globalization and National Economies 1980-2000," 965-966.

27. Martha Honey, *Ecotourism and Sustainable Development: Who Owns Paradise?* Second Edition. (Washington, D.C.: Island Press, 2008), 27.

28. *Instituto Costarricense de Turismo* (ICT), "Costa Rica Tourism Statistical Report", accessed March 12, 2012, http://visitcostarica.com/ict/paginas/statistics/Yearly _2005.pdf.

29. J. S. Akama, and D. M. Kieti, "Tourism and Socio-economic Development in Developing Countries: A Case Study of Mombasa Resort in Kenya," *Journal of Sustainable Tourism,* 15 (2007): 746-747.

30. Joan Giannecchini, "Ecotourism: New Partners, New Relationships," *Conservation Biology* 7 (1993): 30.

31. Weinberg, Bellows and Ekster, "Sustaining Ecotourism: Insights and Implications from Two Successful Case Studies," 375.

32. Honey, *Ecotourism and Sustainable Development: Who Owns Paradise?* Second Edition, 32.

33. Ibid., 114.

34. Wall and Mathieson, *Tourism: Change, Impacts and Opportunities*, 295.

35. Mario A. Boza, "Conservation in Action: Past, Present, and Future of the National Park System of Costa Rica," *Conservation Biology 7* (1993): 247.

36. United Nations Environmental Programme. "Towards a Green Economy: Pathways to Sustainable Development and Poverty Eradication," accessed January 5, 2012, http://www.unep.org/greeneconomy.

37. Honey, *Ecotourism and Sustainable Development: Who Owns Paradise?* Second Edition.

38. Tim Coone, "Costa Rica's 'eco-tourism' helps precious rain forests," *The Financial Post* (Canada), November 13, 1989.

39. Jennifer Blanke and Thea Chiesa, "The Travel & Tourism Competitiveness Report 2007: Furthering the Process of Economic Development," accessed November 5, 2010, http://weforum.org.

40. Tony Binns and Etienne Nel, "Tourism as a local development strategy in South Africa," *The Geographical Journal* 168 (2002) 235.

41. Rosine Hanna and Tugrul U. Daim, "Managing offshore outsourcing in the software industry," *Technology Analysis and Strategic Management* 21 (2009): 895.

42. Shalini Tripathi and Masood H, Siddiqui, "An empirical analysis of tourist preferences using conjoint analysis," *International Journal of Business Science and Applied Management* 5 (2010): 42.

Chapter 2
Politics, Economics and Exceptionalism in Costa Rica

Writing during the Cold War, Robert Wesson referred to Costa Rica as "a civilianist island in a Central America otherwise dominated by military and dictatorial governments."[1] For decades many American as well as Costa Rican scholars have pointed to political culture as the causal variable in Costa Rican exceptionalism. The idea that Costa Rica is different from its neighbors due to its unique history and concurrently unique political culture is also prominent among many Costa Rican citizens. The self-perception among Costa Ricans that they are significantly different from the other peoples of Central America is one of their most important self-identities and this chapter will examine the development of that identity through the lens of Costa Rican exceptionalism. This chapter will also examine the political economic history of Costa Rica and the factors which led to its development, including the way in which Costa Rica's history laid the foundation for the later emergence of ecotourism.

The Building Blocks of Ecotourism

Overall, the trajectory of Costa Rican history created a social and political system that made the underlying factors facilitating ecotourism possible. From the advent of a wage labor system during the colonial period to the construction of Costa Rican nationalism in the nineteenth century, Costa Ricans have long sought ways to stay out of conflict with one another. The underlying cultural norm of accommodation was important during the Great Depression and especially important as the country emerged from its short, but brutal civil war. The settlement of the civil war and the removal of the military from public life in 1949 were the two most significant events in determining modern-day Costa Rica.

These two events essentially constituted the building blocks of economic growth in the post-World War II era and allowed for the construction of the social democratic model, which would play a strong role in creating the post-World War II Costa Rican social and political systems, and would produce a regime with a strong adherence to the rule of law and a desire to build human capital through education. Due to these developments, Costa Rica was well equipped for the installation of neo-liberalism as a result of the structural adjustment policies of the 1980s. The final development that helped to facilitate ecotourism was the emergence of an environmental ethic which stemmed from the overuse of natural resources for much of the twentieth century. Although foreign tourists would not start arriving in large numbers until the 1980s, the underlying conditions that would help to create the ecotourism industry were set in motion early on in Costa Rican history.

Costa Rica and Its Neighbors

A great deal of what underlies Costa Rican self-identity and exceptionalism is what has come to be called the rural democracy thesis. Although it exists with some minor variation, essentially the rural democracy thesis argues that Costa Rican exceptionalism and later adherence to democracy and nonviolence are due in large part to a number of factors that have their origins in the colonial period. These factors include a colonial Costa Rica that was heavily rural and agrarian, democratic in its early stages, racially homogenous due to the lack of a large indigenous population, and poverty stricken. All of these factors dictated that colonial Costa Rica was egalitarian with little economic differentiation between different groups of society.

John A. Booth contends that Costa Rica's perceived difference between itself and its neighbors emerges from the national myth that democracy arose and persists because of "high degrees of social equality, equality of land distribution, racial homogeneity, and a tradition of nonviolence."[2] Since Costa Rican exceptionalism is such an integral part of Costa Rican self-identity it has emerged as one of the guiding principles of the Costa Rican tourism industry which proudly declares Costa Rica to be the "Switzerland of Central America." It is this idea of exceptionalism and what it means to be *tico* that underlies Costa Rican development and many of the differences between Costa Rica and the other states of Central America.

The positive attributes of Costa Rican exceptionalism should also be seen in juxtaposition to other Central American states, which are seen by many Costa Ricans as having a political culture and history that makes them, in many ways, the polar opposite of Costa Rica. To many Costa Ricans, the difference between themselves and Nicaragua is particularly severe, with Nicaragua providing a counterpoint to some of the most dearly held values of what it means to be Costa Rican. According to Carlos Sandoval-Garcia, Nicaragua provides a counterpoint to Costa Rican exceptionalism by representing all of the attributes of Costa Rica in their opposite incarnation. Sandoval-Garcia argues that "the Nicaraguan 'other' is frequently associated with a turbulent political past, dark skin, poverty, and nondemocratic forms of government."[3] Sandoval-Garcia attributes the Costa Rican sense of nationhood to an idyllic past going back to colonialism, racial representations that consider Costa Rica as inhabited by "white" people, and uniqueness of culture as the most prominent factors in the formation of Costa Rican national identity.[4]

Costa Rican nationalism with respect to Nicaragua is particularly heightened in the Guanacaste region of northwest Costa Rica, which was originally the southernmost province of Nicaragua but seceded from Nicaragua to join Costa Rica on July 25, 1824. This secession has an important place in the popular mind of both Guanacastecos and Costa Ricans who saw the secession as evidence that the people of Guanacaste were able to perceive early in Costa Rican history that there were major differences between being Costa Rican or Nicaraguan and that it was preferable to be Costa Rican. July 25th is still celebrated throughout Guanacaste as "Independence Day."

The modern history of Nicaragua, particularly the civil war of the 1980s, has had a major effect on the way that Costa Ricans view Nicaragua, particularly when the turbulence in Nicaraguan politics would spill over into Costa Rica. During the 1979 Sandinista revolution, anti-Sandinista Nicaraguans established a shadow Nicaraguan government in San José. When the Sandinistas prevailed, anti-Sandinista forces fled Nicaragua for Costa Rica in large numbers.

The sense of "otherness" for Nicaraguans is also exacerbated by the relatively high number of Nicaraguans living in Costa Rica who almost exclusively inhabit the lower rungs of Costa Rica society. After Costa Rica's defeat in the 1997 World Cup qualifying game, Costa Rican fans were so incensed that some "renounced" their nationality to become *Nica*.[5] The renunciation of their Costa Rican citizenship was meant to represent just how embarrassing the Costa Rican team's performance had been and they had done so poorly, it was actually less humiliating to be *Nica*.

Marquette found that since the end of the civil war in Nicaragua that Nicaraguans have grown from 2 percent to 6 percent of the population of Costa Rica and tend to be younger, less educated with larger and more complex households.[6] Due to these issues, Nicaraguan immigration to Costa Rica is seen by many Costa Ricans as a significant problem. For instance, President Laura Chinchilla, when she was Costa Rican minister of justice and first vice-president, wrote in the Costa Rican newspaper *La Nación* "the large and uncontrolled increase in the immigrant population in recent years . . . threatens to generate negative pressure on variables such as urban space, employment, the quality and coverage of social services, the rational use of renewable resources, etc."[7]

In order to assess Costa Rican exceptionalism at its roots, as well as the possibility of a Costa Rican model of development and its applicability to other states of Central America, it is necessary to examine the historic foundations of Costa Rican exceptionalism, including the emergence of the rural democracy thesis in the colonial period, the rise of the liberals in the nineteenth century, the aftermath of the Costa Rican civil war and the turn toward neoliberalism in the 1980s and 1990s, and the way in which these events helped to form modern Costa Rica.

Colonial Costa Rica

Many accounts of Costa Rican exceptionalism begin with the idea that Costa Rica was sparsely populated prior to the arrival of the Spaniards. While not as densely populated as many other parts of pre-Columbian Latin America, Costa Rica had a pre-conquest population of about 400,000 inhabitants concentrated in the Northern Pacific Coast and Central Valley.[8] Despite a relatively small number of indigenous peoples, Spain found Costa Rica very difficult to conquer due to the dispersed nature of the population. "Unlike the Incas of South America or the Aztecs of Mexico, Indian society in Central America had no centralized authority . . . as a result no central power source existed that could be conquered."[9] Due to population dispersal patterns, the conquest of Costa Rica had to work piecemeal, one tribe at a time, with no single central authority to defeat. The population density of the native population also affected the rate at which the population diminished over time. Kramer notes that "in areas with low-density native populations . . . the Indians diminished rapidly in the years immediately following Spanish conquest."[10]

The relationship between the Indians and Spaniards was greatly influenced by the native institutions the conquistadores found when they arrived in the "New World." Native groups who were accustomed to tribute and labor expectations, such as the Aztecs, who had an extensive tribute system among those they had conquered, transitioned much more easily to Spanish colonialism than groups who were isolated and sparse. The sparseness of the native population coupled with the lack of a pre-colonial tribute system meant that the relatively small native population was in some ways more difficult to conquer than the much more densely populated areas. The difficulty of conquering the native population led to a great deal of consternation among the early conquistadores. As one conquistador famously complained to the Spanish Crown "Your majesty may be assured that in Costa Rica there are no peaceful Indians."[11]

Despite the difficulties of conquest and similar to other indigenous populations throughout Latin America, the indigenous population in Costa Rica saw a rapid decline, from 400,000 in 1502 to 120,000 in 1576 to 10,000 in 1611 due to war, exploitation, and disease.[12] By the mid-seventeenth century the indigenous population in Costa Rica was so small that in 1677 the treasurer refused to give the governor 161 pesos "to embark on a campaign to take out Indians," instead funneling money toward a war with France and Britain.[13] In other words, the threat from the indigenous population by this time was so small that money could not be spared for campaigns against them.

The rapid decline and near extinction of the indigenous population helps to explain why Costa Ricans have traditionally believed that they have inherited an "empty" country. Costa Rica was essentially "cleared" of its indigenous population, and population growth did not restart until about 1750, with the mestizo population growing from 4 percent to 58 percent of the population during the eighteenth century.[14] The mestizoization of Costa Rica and the lack of a large indigenous population that could be exploited for its labor had an important effect on the formation of a wage labor system in Costa Rica. The Costa Rican workforce "was not made up of a conquered race or of imported slaves held in inferior status by the institutionalized tyranny of a ruling class, but of persons accustomed to being free and who had the same cultural heritage as the emerging coffee barons."[15]

The colonial relationship of a free, mestizo labor class to Costa Rican elites is considerably different than the relationship between the indigenous population and elites in countries such as Guatemala and El Salvador. The later relationship between labor, elites, and the state was shaped during the pre-colonial and colonial period and is important for understanding modern Costa Rica. In order to discern the differences between the colonial experience of Costa Rica and other parts of colonial Latin America, it is important to first briefly discuss the encomienda and later repartimiento systems of labor and the variations across colonial Latin America.

The Encomienda and Repartimiento in Spanish America

When the conquistadores first conquered the Caribbean and then moved to mainland Latin America, one of the first problems they encountered when trying to sustain themselves and rule was the severe shortage of labor. With relatively few conquistadores it was necessary for them to find a way to exploit the labor of the native population in order to establish a working and profitable colony. It was out of this desire that the encomienda system was created. The encomienda system in colonial Latin America gave conquistadores the labor they needed to work the land, but did not grant the land itself. The encomienda was "a formal grant of designated Indian families, usually the inhabitants of a town or a cluster of towns, entrusted to the charge of a Spanish colonist who thus became encomendero."[16] The population transferred to the encomendero was a source of cheap labor to be exploited. In addition, the indigenous people who found themselves a part of the encomienda system were also expected to pay tribute to their encomendero in food or other locally produced goods. In many ways the encomienda was the importation of feudal Europe to the "New World," as the encomendero received tribute from the Indian population in exchange for providing the Indian population "protection and instruction in the Catholic faith."[17] The right of encomienda was commonly used as a reward for conquistadores who helped to subdue the area. The idea of encomienda as reward for service was "fixed in conquistadores' minds as an appropriate, if not indispensable, reward for their actions."[18] Sometimes an encomienda was even granted before an area was subdued in order to provide the appropriate motivation among the conquistadores who expected to be rewarded when the campaign was finished.[19]

In addition to the exploitation of native labor by the Spaniards, there were also fundamental cultural misunderstandings with respect to work and wages. When the

Spaniards began to govern their newly conquered territories they thought the native population would gladly come to them for work in order to get paid. This was a cultural misinterpretation, however, because as a subsistence society the Indians did not come from the same capitalist mind-set as the Spaniards and therefore did not have the same desire for money and accumulation. The populations conquered by the Spaniards had engaged almost exclusively in the barter system and did not have much concern for money, which was for them essentially a foreign concept.

The cultural difference with respect to wage labor not only made early Spanish labor systems difficult to manage, it also helped to establish a difficult relationship very early between the conquistadores and the Indian population. Obviously, the vast majority of the people who were vanquished by the conquistadores and were forced to labor for them, did not do so willingly. "The Indians, were loath to perform these functions voluntarily, and had to be enslaved and forced to provide food and gold for the Spaniards."[20] The installation of the encomienda meant that the Spaniards began to enslave the indigenous population throughout Latin America from the very outset of colonization. The enslavement of the Indian population and their use as labor helped to establish a precedent whereby one of the most desirable "payoffs" for a conquistador was access to encomienda labor, therefore making areas that had a large indigenous population very desirable to conquer.

Due to its relative lack of exploitable resources in relation to other parts of colonial Latin America, most of colonial Central America, with the exception of Guatemala, was seen as a backwater to the larger and much more important area of New Spain, now modern Mexico. Even within the peripheral areas of Spanish colonialism there were regional variations of colonial importance and a consequent deviation in the substance and form of encomienda. Guatemala, for instance, suffered from greater exploitation due to its gold placer mines and because it was a route to other places in Central America and, most importantly the Vice Royalty of Peru.[21] A major factor to Guatemala being more heavily exploited was the perception among conquistadores of the possibility for great riches if a colonist could get an assignment there and the establishment of an encomienda in Guatemala became a source of great contention and for many Spaniards "the Guatemalan encomienda was quickly established and immediately became the focus of strong competition between rival colonists."[22]

This competition between rival colonists also helped to engender lawlessness as individuals competed for encomiendas and other benefits to be had from colonizing Guatemala. "In Guatemala, the encomienda was shaped, not by laws so much as by local conditions and the virtually unchecked control which local governors exercised in the first twenty years of Spanish colonization."[23] This lawlessness helped to shape the relationship between the indigenous population and the Spaniards by engendering a number of uprisings. It would also serve to create a relationship between labor and elites that would persist for centuries and in some places still flourishes to the present day.

In many ways the lives of those exploited for labor in the encomienda system was harsher than those who were imported as slaves. While the slaves were the property of the slave owner, the Indians engaged in forced labor were a grant to be used and discarded. Additionally, while slaves were provided with the most basic needs, the Indians used for forced labor were required to procure, among other things, their own food. The Indians in the encomienda became a sort of "commons" to be used and discarded while slaves were property that had to be afforded at least a minimum level of protection and care due to the cost involved in acquiring them.

The growing power of the encomenderos and the vast distance between Spain and the New World made any enforcement of restrictions on the use of encomienda labor very difficult. One of the ways in which the Crown attempted to give force to the restrictions of the use of Indian labor came with a series of laws enacted in 1542 known as the New Laws of the Indies for the Good Treatment and Preservation of the Indians. For the most part, the Spanish Crown's concern over the encomienda system was borne out of its anxiety over encomenderos becoming too powerful and wealthy rather than any concern for the welfare of the Indian population. In the *New Laws* the Crown restricted Indian labor in three important ways in order to further differentiate encomienda Indians from slaves:

1. Indians were not owned by encomenderos and could therefore not be bought, sold, or rented to others.
2. Encomenderos were forbidden inheritance rights and encomiendas did not automatically transfer to future generations.
3. Indians could not be relocated from their proximate geographical area.[24]

The New Laws and other attempts to enforce restrictions on the use of encomienda labor also helped to foster a rift between the Crown and colonists. The struggle between the Crown who favored those born in Spain, known as peninsulares, and the colonists, known as criollos, who wanted to be autonomous was one of the first signs of the conflict between those in the "New World" and those in Spain that would plague elite relations in Spanish America for the remainder of colonialism and would serve as one of the underlying causes of the wars of revolution in Latin America centuries later.

Despite the true motivation of the Spanish crown, most scholars agree that the plight of the indigenous population in Spanish America was better in 1600 than it had been in the first few decades of the sixteenth century. However, the enactment and implementation of the New Laws and attempts to stop or reform the encomienda system was in large part a struggle between the Spanish crown and the growing power of those who controlled land and labor in the colonies. Many encomenderos protested vehemently when the crown tried to reform the encomienda, arguing that without Indian labor they would no longer be able to sustain themselves. Due to this power struggle and the difficulty on the part of the crown to control the encomenderos, Caporossi argues that the encomienda survived in general until the end of the eighteenth century and in some cases until the wars of revolution.[25] The "on paper" reform and decline of the encomienda meant that colonial authorities needed to find a new way to continue providing the labor required to sustain their operations, which was found in the repartimiento.

When the Crown was finally able to somewhat alter the practice of encomienda it did not mean the end of forced labor for the indigenous population. Sources of labor were necessary not only due to the Spaniards desire for cheap exploitable labor to sustain their operations, but also because of the Spanish belief that the Indians were inherently lazy and had to be forced to work for their own good. Due to this "the Spanish and creole elites, the Indians and the state worked out a forced wage labor system, called variously repartimientos or mitas."[26] The repartimiento system worked in the following manner:

> Each native village was notified to send a certain number of men to a Spanish town every week. They were to assemble in the main plaza every Monday morning to be assigned for the week's work. The workers were then divided up according to the labor demands, either for public-works projects of for the use of individual Spaniards who had submitted requests for a stated number of laborers.[27]

Obviously the labor requirements put on villages were often odious and even after the practice had become customary it was widely despised by the Indian population. One report from the time states that on the day the laborers reported for work "it seems more as if they were going to prison or to the gallows."[28] In addition, as some villages suffered from a steep decline in population, the repartimiento exacted a much larger percent of the population than it had intended to on paper.

> Depending on custom and conditions, a village might be required to supply anywhere from 7 percent to 25 percent of its repartimiento eligible population for forced wage labor, for periods of a week to a year or more. Of course, censuses fell out of date, particularly in the wake of an epidemic or large scale migration. Because Crown agents were loath to recognize this and slow to carry out new counts, what was on paper a quarter of the population might, in fact, amount to a half or more of the surviving workers in a given town. Repartimiento labor was paid labor, but it was forced labor, and the wages generally were below those of the free market.[29]

These labor systems, which existed throughout most of Spanish colonialism, were highly exploitative and brutal systems of labor which existed from first contact through independence, though in some places the same patterns of behavior persisted even after the Spaniards left. The rural democracy thesis rests on the idea that the difference in colonial experience led the countries of Central America down different historical paths, which are still very different today.

Colonial Labor Practices and the Rural Democracy Thesis

Even with many reforms to colonial labor practices, the pattern of labor relations between the elite and masses had been set early in the colonial period. "The progression from encomienda to repartimiento/mita to free wage labor (was) the classic pattern of labor institutions in Spanish America."[30] One of the primary differences between Costa Rica and the rest of Central America was the more compressed nature of this pattern because Costa Rica moved much more quickly to free wage labor than its neighbors. This would greatly impact the way in which Costa Rica would develop.

The nature and legacy of the labor and economic arrangements of colonial era Costa Rica has been a source of great debate among scholars. Harrison goes so far as to say that the Costa Rican colonial experience created a significant modification to the mainstream of Hispanic-American culture and that colonial Costa Rica is in some ways reminiscent of colonial New England. He also attributes the historic problems of Nicaragua as being due to its colonial past in the mainstream of Hispanic-American culture.[31] These comparisons with Costa Rica as the outlier of "mainstream" Central American history and culture are a common theme in much of the rural democracy thesis literature.

As a result, many scholars have argued for the rural democracy thesis as an explanation for the development of Costa Rican democracy including, Carlos Monge Alfaro,[32] Mitchell A. Seligson,[33] Charles D. Ameringer,[34] Lawrence E. Harrison,[35] and Samuel Stone.[36] Although with some variation, most adherents to this idea argue that due to the difficult terrain and the relative lack of exploitable natural resources, the Costa Rican colonial experience was vastly different from that of its neighbors. This difference in colonial experience helps to explain why Costa Rica has been able to build a stable democracy in a region where dictatorship and political instability have been the norm.

Due to the lack of resources and the sparseness of the indigenous population, Costa Rica was one of the last parts of Spanish America to be settled. This lack of resources also meant that Costa Rica (during the colonial period) was not an attractive place for wealthy Spaniards to settle. "Costa Rica lacked sufficient mineral wealth to attract the gold seekers, and its indigenous population was too small to permit the establishment of large landed estates."[37] Wealthy Spaniards were much more likely to settle in places like central Mexico with its large indigenous population or Peru with its large source of exploitable mineral wealth. Consequently, Costa Rica attracted a different type of settler because of the absence of easy sources of income.

According to Seligson, the absence of gold and a small Indian population along with geographic isolation led to a land tenure system in Costa Rica that facilitated the creation of a large yeoman class rather than a large hacienda system.[38] As discussed above, much of Latin America had its labor relations affected by the early encomienda and repartimiento systems, which influenced the relations between elites and the masses for centuries. The early failures as well as the small indigenous population helped to move Costa Rica more quickly to a system of free wage labor.

The early development of a large yeoman class also differentiates Costa Rica from other parts of the Spanish colonial system because there was not the extreme differentiation between economic classes like in other parts of Spanish America. Although it cannot be argued that Costa Rica was some sort of egalitarian paradise, it is important to acknowledge the differences in economic differentiation between Costa Rica and its neighbors as a matter of degree. While there was economic differentiation between Costa Ricans, it was not as sharp as other parts of Central America and therefore does not serve as the defining characteristic between the elite and masses as it does in countries such as Nicaragua, Guatemala, or El Salvador, whose labor relations still suffer from issues of race, ethnicity and social class as well as a persistent feeling that the conquerors are still ruling the conquered.

What emerges is a system in which Seligson argues the major distinction was social rather than economic.[39] The lack of large-scale economic differentiation helped to create a pattern of labor relations very different from other parts of Spanish colonialism and provides a start to understanding why labor relations in Costa Rica differ so extensively from labor relations in countries such as Guatemala and El Salvador. That is not to say that there were no rich people in colonial Costa Rica, but that the income gap between rich and poor was not as disparate as it was in other parts of Spanish America. The lack of resources and easy paths to wealth for the Spaniards had a large impact on the development of Costa Rica.

During Spanish colonialism, the primary differences between Costa Rica and its neighbors was the lack of resources, the development of free labor and the effect these had on the early creation of the way the elite and masses relate to one another. For instance, Seligson argues that had some means of extracting wealth been uncovered in the colony, the Crown and the local aristocracy would have forced the peasants to do the extracting. The lack of easily exploitable resources, while bad for the aristocracy, was good for the rest of the population because peasants were able to settle small plots of land with little interference.[40] While some large plots existed in colonial Costa Rica, it is this small-scale settlement and the nature of labor relations, especially the fact that a wage labor system rather than a slave labor system, that differentiated the Costa Rican colonial experience from other parts of Latin America.

The lack of easily exploitable resources also meant that the modest living standards of colonial Costa Rica extended to the highest levels of the colonial administration. For example, the colonial governor reported in 1719 that he would have to do his own sowing and reaping or he would perish.[41] Due to the harshness of life in colonial Costa Rica, some scholars argue that it attracted a different type of colonist. "Colonists were by self-selection different from the conquistadores, they had to work the land themselves if they were to survive, and survival was a pressing issue for virtually everyone."[42]

More recent scholarship, however, has begun to chip away at many important aspects of the rural democracy thesis and has questioned many of its base assumptions. Alternatives to the cultural argument inherent in the rural democracy thesis have included scholars who have attributed Costa Rican democracy to institutional factors, such as Wilson,[43] Lehoucq,[44] or structural and elite settlement factors, such as Booth.[45] These arguments have tended to differ from the rural democracy thesis by either reinterpreting Costa Rican history or by finding the explanatory factors of modern Costa Rican politics much later in Costa Rican history than previous scholars.

Lowell Gudmundson has provided the most strident critique of the rural democracy thesis. He argues that pre-coffee Costa Rican village society was based on nucleated rather than dispersed settlements as the rural democracy thesis argues. "The importance of this unusual settlement pattern (nucleated villages) lies in its relationship to historically formed social-control mechanisms in both Spain and colonial Spanish America."[46] Gudmundson also argues that land was not appropriated by small holders who worked the land at a subsistence level but instead land tenure fell into three specific types: The non-private cultivation of common lands, small holdings on the village outskirts by non -residents, and the ownership of large estates by the wealthy.

Gudmundson's critique is important because it serves to somewhat demystify Costa Rica's history and provides a more nuanced look at pre-coffee Costa Rica than the rural democracy thesis alone can provide. Gudmundson also rightly points out that much of the development of the rural democracy thesis came from the Generation of 48 in order to have a rallying point for the people after the 1948 Costa Rican civil war. "The originators of the rural democratic model forged their ideas in the process of nationalistic renewal and sociopolitical conflict."[47]

While Costa Rican politicians have for decades used the rural democracy thesis and its logical derivations for nationalist and at times even xenophobic ends what is important to understand about the colonial period in Costa Rican history is that it falls somewhere between the violent and hugely differentiated experience of Spanish colonialism experienced throughout the region and the mythic utopian Costa Rica promulgated by many who advocate the rural democracy thesis.

Some scholars who are critical of the rural democracy thesis confirm aspects of the argument (such as Booth, for example) argue that aspects of Costa Rican colonial life may have contributed to the eventual development of democracy. These factors include the lack of highly concentrated land ownership, low levels of economic differentiation among the people, and Costa Rica's isolation which gave the political elite some experience with governing.[48] Democracy was able to develop in Costa Rica because the lack of resources meant that the early race for land and wealth was more equitable in Costa Rica than in other parts of the region. Thus, as Seligson points out "largely as a result of the crushing poverty of the colony, Costa Rica's evolution was markedly different from that of her neighbors."[49]

Independence and the Central American Federal Republic

Independence came to Costa Rica when Mexico split from Spain in 1821 and took with it the Audencia of Guatemala which included all of Central America. Similarly to the colonial period, Costa Rica's remoteness from the center of politics would have an effect on how it developed. "As Guatemala's most distant region, Costa Rica's colonial status ended without any local combat."[50] The period of Central American inclusion in the Mexican empire lasted until 1823 when Costa Rica declared its sovereignty, broke from Mexico and joined Guatemala, El Salvador, Honduras, and Nicaragua in the newly created Central American Federal Republic (CAF).

From the beginning, the CAF was rife with a number of elite conflicts, some of which had their roots in the colonial period such as the rivalry between criollos and peninsulares which was "produced by the rules and regulations that surrounded the colonial administration (that) excluded Spaniards born in Latin America from holding profitable and prestigious administrative positions."[51] The other key elite conflict of the post-independence period was between the liberal faction which backed a continuation of the earlier Bourbon reforms and centered much of their ideology on a state free from clerical interference and economic development based on exports and conservatives who advocated a continuation of the major institutions from the colonial period, most especially a powerful Catholic Church. In Central America, like in much of Latin America, the struggle between liberals and conservatives during this period created a great deal of conflict which would help to usher in long periods of military rule throughout the region. Costa Rica however was largely immune to the negative effects of the liberal/conservative struggle, as Booth points out "except in Costa Rica, continued liberal-conservative factionalism, forced indigenous labor, and the hacienda system all contributed to a strong political role for the region's militaries."[52]

While the elite of other Central American states were fighting over how to divide the spoils of the CAF among themselves, Costa Rica largely lay outside the squabble and concentrated on creating Costa Rican nationalism, even though they were still a small, poor, and politically unstable state. For instance, in the same year the CAF was founded (1821), Costa Rica signed the Pact of Harmony which institutionalized an itinerant government which obligated high officials to reside in each of the country's four major cities for a part of the year. This served to divide up equally the prestige and power attached to the seat of government.[53] To this day, Costa Rican presidents do not live in a government subsidized residence, but instead are responsible for their own lodging in San José during their term. Evidence of building Costa Rican nationalism and their own perception that they are different from their neighbors is inherent in the belief among Costa Rican elites of the time that were concerned over the direction of the CAF and how the "innately peaceful" Costa Ricans might be infected by the behavior of other CAF members, thus squelching their own perceived innate peacefulness. In 1830, an unnamed Costa Rican politician would give one of the first expressions of the idea that Costa Ricans think of themselves as different from their neighbors:

> Costa Rica has set a good example in every respect for the other states of the (CAF). It is neither reasonable nor just that Costa Rica should now lose the beautiful prestige that it has earned through its constant vigilance in the protection of harmony, its exact adherence to the law, and its continuous repudiation of the partisan rows and personalist ideas that have been in abundant evidence in the other states.[54]

The isolation from the CAF's seat of government in Guatemala as well as the indifference of Costa Rican leaders to the organization also helped to separate Costa Rica from the conflict among the other states. While the historical currents and ideological battles present in the CAF were also present in Costa Rica, Costa Rican leaders dealt with these issues differently which led to a different outcome, particularly with Juan Mora Fernández who was the Costa Rican head of state from 1824-1833. Mora paid little heed to the CAF and instead concentrated on nation-building, including the creation of a national flag, coat of arms and the incorporation of many cities and towns.[55]

Costa Rican isolation from the center of politics, whether it was during Spanish colonialism, as a part of Mexico, or as a member of the CAF, helped to create a Costa Rican elite that had some experience with governance. The elite's experience with governance played an important role in the collapse of the CAF in 1839, which can ultimately be attributed to the liberal-conservative split and Costa Rican perceptions of the differences between themselves and the other CAF countries.

The Development of Coffee as an Export Crop

Soon after leaving the CAF, the coffee trade would establish itself as Costa Rica's most important export. The development of coffee as an export crop had a profound effect on the historical development of Central America and was long been at center of Costa Rican consciousness. Starting with the opening of the European market to Costa Rican coffee in the mid-nineteenth century, coffee quickly became the major source of foreign exchange in Costa Rica easily outpacing other traditional exports such as bananas or beans. Affectionately known as *grano de oro*, the high profitability of coffee placed it at the center of the Costa Rican economy and it fueled Costa Rican economic growth for most of the nineteenth century, serving as "the principle engine of economic growth and social change for a century."[56] Coffee continued to maintain its hold on the Costa Rican economy for more than a century, only declining in value relative to other economic pursuits starting in the 1960s. Even with the relative decline in the importance of coffee to the Costa Rican economy, coffee growers still warmly refer to the centrality of "coffee culture" in Costa Rican public life.

The centrality of coffee to the Costa Rican economy had a number of important ramifications for development. The high profitability and concurrent reliance on coffee exportation as the centerpiece of a commodity-driven export model helped to establish Costa Rica in a peripheral position to the world economy. As a country peripheral to the world economy, Costa Rica was highly vulnerable to the ebb and flow of the world commodity market and the inevitable problems that would occur. Chief among them was the problem of declining terms of trade that resulted from the price inequality of Costa Rican agricultural exports sold in order to buy the continually pricier manufactured goods from the developed world.

Also problematic was the concentration of coffee production into the hands of a relatively few cafetaleros, which helped to increase inequality across Costa Rican society. Although Costa Rican coffee production has traditionally not been as highly concentrated as it is in other parts of Central America, there were still a few prominent families that dominated Costa Rican coffee production over the course of several centuries. Many Costa Rican coffee elites are even able to trace their lineage to an individual conquistador. For example, one of Costa Rica's most famous coffee dynasties, the Montealegres, are direct descendants of conquistador Juan Vázquez de Coronado. José Maria, the founder of the coffee dynasty, became president of Costa Rica in 1860 via a coup d'état which deposed another cafétalero whose plans threatened the Montealegres.[57] The Montealegres were not alone in their desire to guide the Costa Rican state apparatus toward policies that would advance the fortunes of the coffee elite and consequently nineteenth-century Costa Rican politics were dominated by politicians from important coffee-growing families.

Even with the dominance of the coffee elite in Costa Rica and throughout Central America, nineteenth-century Costa Rica showed signs of a latent democracy absent in other places "elections—albeit indirect, elite-dominated and sometimes fraudulent—became an important facet of Costa Rican politics."[58] While elections were often fraudulent, the elite-dominated electoral veneer was an important sign of the differences between the Costa Rican elite and other elites from throughout Central America who did not even bother having minimal democracy. For instance, when comparing the ruling coffee elite in Costa Rica to the coffee elite of El Salvador, the differences between the two are quite pronounced. The fundamental difference between the Costa Rican and Salvadoran coffee elite was the relationship between the elites and workers, particularly the use of the military to control labor. The coffee elite in Costa Rica never adopted military guaranteed forced labor because it would have been very difficult to implement due to the availability of land, therefore growers were forced to pay high wages in order to attract workers.[59] The difference in historical narrative between the relatively highly paid worker in Costa Rica, whose position was somewhat secure due to the structure of Costa Rican colonial economy, and those who worked under a system of military guaranteed labor is immense.

An illustration of this difference is the so-called marriage of convenience between Salvadoran coffee growers and the military, each of which used their own power to reinforce the power of the other. This close association between the coffee elite and military meant that El Salvador endured a long history of military guaranteed labor that helped to put a wedge between social classes early in Salvadoran history and played an integral role in the development of Salvadoran politics and society, and, as Paige points out, was one of the underlying causes of the Salvadoran civil war of the 1980s.[60]

Guatemala is another country with a long history of military guaranteed labor. "The Guatemalan state deployed a coercive military apparatus to control or quash political and social organizing, to promote land concentration, and to deliver labor to coffee plantations."[61] The Guatemalan state even went as far as to reinstate the labor practices of Spanish colonialism at the behest of the coffee elite when it reestablished repartimiento labor which had been outlawed at independence in 1876.[62] There are also differences between the nature of the economic activities of the Guatemalan and Costa Rican coffee elite. While the Guatemalan coffee elite were made up primarily of coffee growers, the Costa Rican elite were made up primarily of coffee processors. This is important due to the nature of the differences between agricultural production and processing. In particular the development of land distribution because of the need for large tracts of land for coffee production, something that is not necessary for processing. The focus on coffee processing among the Costa Rican elite meant that they required neither the extensive labor nor substantial tracts of land like the other coffee-producing states of Central America.

As a result, for Costa Rican coffee production there was a tendency for small- and medium-sized coffee plantations rather than large-scale haciendas. That is not to say that large operations did not exist in Costa Rica, but those small- and medium-sized operations had a larger percentage of the total output than the other coffee-producing states. As Paige argues, when compared to El Salvador and Nicaragua, the small-holding coffee farmer in Costa Rica controlled a much larger share of coffee area and production which reflects substantial differences in the political power of the large land-holding coffee elite in El Salvador and Nicaragua.[63] The preeminence of large estates in Nicaragua and El Salvador meant that power and wealth were much more concentrated than they were in Costa Rica. The smaller scale of Costa Rican coffee farming also contributed to the absence of military guaranteed labor because of the more diffuse nature of Costa Rican coffee production which in turn meant that the less powerful small- and medium-sized growers did not have the power or resources to call on the military for help.

The lack of military guaranteed labor in Costa Rica also meant that they did not have the long and ingrained history of military involvement in the affairs of the economic elite. This allowed for a much different outlook among Costa Rican elite, especially when compared to the coffee elite of El Salvador and Guatemala. As Yashar points out, "the Costa Rican state did not actively repress the population in the name of the agrarian elites."[64] Consequently, the relationship between the economic elite, the state, and the general population developed in a different manner in Costa Rica than in many of the other coffee-growing states of Central

America and Costa Rica would not experience the high levels of social class tension endured by many of its neighbors.

Crises of the 1930s

Similarly to any economy that relies heavily on agro-exports, the Great Depression and subsequent crash of the commodities market hit Costa Rica very hard. The international coffee market was especially hard hit and "in 1930 prices for Costa Rican coffee dropped by one-third from their highs in the late 1920s."[65] Throughout Central America, the Great Depression and steep decline in the price of coffee led to a great deal of unrest among workers and a significant increase in membership in Marxist-oriented political movements which would apply similar political and economic pressure to states across Central America. The manner in which the elites and society at large would filter and act upon the conditions would differ greatly across the region and marks the beginning of the large difference between Costa Rica and its neighbors. For instance, Paige argues that the crises of the 1930s and the ideological conflict between the coffee elite and insurrection movements is fundamental to understanding the later differences in the politics (and conflicts) of the 1980s between Costa Rica and states such as El Salvador and Nicaragua.[66]

The difference between the elite response to the Great Depression and the concurrent leftist mobilization is again the most divergent when comparing Costa Rica to El Salvador. While both countries experienced similar political and economic problems, their responses were conditioned by the manner in which each society had been constructed. In El Salvador, the legacy of colonialism was military guaranteed labor and a large economic and social divide between the elite and masses while in Costa Rica the legacy of colonialism was a much less oppressive labor system and consequently much better, though not perfect, relations between the elite and masses emerged. The differences in the development of each country would manifest itself in the manner in which the elites reacted to popular mobilization. The Costa Rican elite dealt with citizen unrest and a burgeoning leftist movement in the same way that it had dealt with political threats since the mid-nineteenth century, by denying them a place in public life; including denying them the ability to run for national office or firing anyone whose loyalty was in question.

Throughout the 1930s and 1940s, the Costa Rican government engaged in such activities as using state employees to spy on the opposition, the firing of all officials loyal to others, and the installation of officials who were loyal to the regime."[67] In contrast to 1930s El Salvador, the differences in elite attitude toward workers become readily apparent. At the same time that the Costa Rican state was spying on and firing those that opposed it, the Salvadoran state was killing the opposition. One of the worst offenses occurred in 1932 when the Salvadoran regime killed between 10,000 and 30,000 Salvadorans during a worker's revolt.[68] This event, which has come to be known in Salvadoran history as *La Matanza,* had an enormous effect on Salvadoran society and represents the height of state-sponsored violence to provide military guaranteed labor. As Anderson points out "the whole political labyrinth of El Salvador can be explained only in reference to the traumatic experience of the uprising and the *matanza*."[69]

One factor which facilitated the somewhat muted response of the Costa Rican government to the rise of the left during the Great Depression was the moderate form of leftist politics in the country. The left in Costa Rica bore little resemblance to the left in either El Salvador or Nicaragua and was much less confrontational. For instance, Costa Rican Communist leader Manuel Mora stated in 1937 that "if it were necessary to 'destroy liberty and all of those attributes of the human personality' in order to realize Marxist doctrine then he 'would be the principle adversary of socialism.'"[70] What Mora set out to create was not a Marxist regime, but instead a social democracy. Mora's moderation and influence over the direction of the Costa Rican government had a profound impact on Costa Rica's future. Mora is also unique among Central American Communist leaders because he survived the conflicts of the 1930s and saw many of his ideas come to fruition.

The 1948 Civil War and Its Aftermath

While the experience of Costa Rica during the Great Depression was milder than its neighbors, economic crisis coupled with an increase in labor strife and the social turmoil it created, meant that the 1930s and 1940s were a time of great disruption in Costa Rica, culminating in the civil war of 1948. The Costa Rican civil war, subsequent settlement and constitution that followed are important factors that differentiate Costa Rica from its neighbors. Particularly important to the future of Costa Rica was the abolishment of the military. With the abolition of the military, Costa Rica took a step that was unimaginable at the time, but would set Costa Rica down its final path toward the creation of a state and society that are divergent from not only its immediate neighbors, but from all of Latin America. This divergence would be institutionalized by the 1949 constitution. Brian Loveman argues that Costa Rican exceptionalism with respect to the constitution comes from a myriad of factors, such as:

> more stringent legislative controls over the executive, a clearer separation of legislative and executive authority, a requirement for three-fourths votes in the legislature to impose regimes of exception and Costa Rican refusal to constitutionalize a political mission for the armed forces distinguished the country's political system from those of the rest of the region.[71]

The abolition of the military would also help to correct a long-standing problem in the development of Costa Rican democracy, the lack of mass political participation. One of the major issues that led to the civil war was the need for electoral reform in order to halt widespread fraud in the electoral system. The abolition of the military was a major factor that helped to increase political participation. "Demilitarization contributed to broadened citizen participation in voter registration and voter turnout in elections after 1949."[72] The Costa Rican constitution was also unusual for Latin America because it limited the powers of the presidency. For instance, the president of Costa Rica has limited veto power, needs two-thirds of the legislature to assume emergency powers, cannot legislate by decree and is limited to one term.[73] One of the most important figures in the time after the civil war was José Figueres Ferrer. The election of Figueres in 1952 helped to bring normalcy back to Costa Rican politics as he "stimulated agricultural exports and negotiated a new contract with United Fruit, under which the Costa Rican share of profits increased from 10 to 30 percent."[74] He also helped to consolidate Costa Rican democracy by presiding over the post-civil war electoral system which over time was able to win the support of the Costa Rican people because of the transparency and fairness of elections. He proved his dedication to democratic politics when his party's candidate lost in the 1958 election and the transfer of power went smoothly, something which was not always the case in Latin American elections. Such a smooth transition of power was evident as Figueres himself pointed out "I consider our defeat as a contribution, in a way, to democracy in Latin America. It is not customary for a party in power to lose an election."[75] The most important lasting legacy of the post-civil war development model were the seeds it would sow for later Costa Rican development since it "emphasized human capital development, closing the urban-rural gap, and concern for the lower and middle classes (which) paid off handsomely in economic, social, and political terms."[76]

Post-World War II Economic Development

Aided by the growth of the developed world predicated on post-World War II rebuilding, the Costa Rican economy took off in the 1950s and grew rapidly throughout the 1960s and 1970s with GDP growth of 27 percent during the 1960s and 31 percent during the 1970s.[77] During this period, the Costa Rican government took an activist approach in subsidizing and nationalizing industry as well as redistributing the benefits of growth. It was also able to capitalize on the post-World War II economic boom through a social democratic development model based on a strategy of import substitution industrialization (ISI), protectionism, government involvement in the economy, and a sizable welfare state. The era of import-substitution industrialization began with the 1959 Industrial Protection Law which "increased tariffs on many imported items and offered industrialists exemptions of virtually 100 percent on local, import, and export taxes."[78] By the early 1960s, Costa Rican economic policy, along with many countries throughout Latin America, had implemented economic models that included import sub-stitution industrialization along with the formation of regional common markets.

These policies were greatly influenced by the memory of the Great Depression and the consequences of reliance on a small number of agricultural exports and the influence of the United Nations Economic Commission for Latin America (ECLA) which strongly advocated a more inward-looking economic model. The highly influential director of ECLA, Raúl Prebisch, argued that the economic structure of the developing world was too highly dependent on agricultural exports and manufacturing imports from the developed world and that this dependence created a pattern of trade that was not beneficial to development. Due to this dynamic, Prebisch advocated that poor countries minimize trade with the developed world in order to build their own industries and trade amongst themselves.[79]

Even as ISI spread across Latin America, there was resistance in Costa Rica to any measure that minimized the role of agricultural exports in the economy, particularly coffee. Although coffee had long been a powerful force in Costa Rica, with every president from 1870-1948 being a member of the coffee elite,[80] the time after the civil war was very difficult for many Costa Rican coffee farmers. Beginning with the dissolution of the army after the 1948 civil war, an institution that had long assisted them in power, the cafetaleros suffered a number of setbacks to their economic power. The other blow was the expanding power of the Social Democrats in government who wanted to deliver on their promise of enlarging the welfare state and who saw the coffee industry as a source of tax revenue. Given the historic power of the coffee elite, they also strongly desired an overall reduction in the economic power of the largest coffee enterprises. As a result, in 1952 the government passed a tax that lowered the allowable profit rate from 16 to 9 percent of total sales and required them to pay a 5 percent tax.[81]

With the coffee industry clearly in their sights, the downturn of the market in the late 1950s, just as ISI was gaining steam throughout the region, provided political cover for Costa Rican politicians who had advocated a move toward industrialization throughout the 1950s. The creation of the Central American Common Market (CACM) in 1960 gave structure to the government's plan and a new outlet for exports. The CACM, which protected Costa Rican industry from products outside the regional trade block and provided a ready market for Costa Rican goods, helped to create an economic base that allowed the Social Democrats to create a substantial welfare state. The social democratic model helped to improve the well-being of citizens and strengthened the state, decreased income inequality, and improved real wages, infant mortality, literacy, life expectancy, and educational attainment.[82] It also provided the basis for an emerging Costa Rican middle-class who would be the first customers of the ecotourism industry as they found themselves with the time and money to pursue leisure activities.

Although the CACM was ultimately a failure, this period in Costa Rica not only helped to increase the importance of industry, but is also indicative of government's attempts after the civil war to decrease the importance of coffee as an export crop. Both industrialization and the government's desire to move beyond coffee as the centerpiece of the export industry would have important effects on later attempts to build an ecotourism industry. Early industrialization would provide investment in infrastructure and services that would be utilized by ecotourism and the government's general desire to increase the support for nontraditional exports would be an important impetus for government policy that supported ecotourism development. The CACM was an important step in the economic development of Costa Rica because it "brought foreign aid to improve roads, ports, and public services"[83] all of which would later play an important role in the development of ecotourism. Interestingly, while the implementation of ISI and the decline of the coffee industry would help to set the stage for ecotourism development, the ultimate collapse of ISI and the social democratic model it helped to create would provide the basis for the development of ecotourism.

The Crisis of the 1980s

By the late 1970s the Costa Rican development model was starting to run out of steam and a number of problems began to emerge. Although by this time Costa Rican exports were somewhat more diversified, the main problem was the intensification of increasingly adverse terms of trade due to the falling prices for Costa Rican exports, with coffee once again at the center. The falling price of Costa Rican exports, coupled with the increased costs of manufactured imports and oil quickly put Costa Rica into economic crisis. The problem of declining terms of trade quickly began to require major changes to the Costa Rican economic model, changes which were difficult to make due to the standard of living that Costa Ricans had become accustomed to and the sacrifices that would therefore be necessary. Due to the strong impact that a new economic model would have on the lifestyles of average Costa Ricans, the government decided instead to borrow large sums of money from international lenders to prop up the now failed social democratic model. Because of the severity of the economic crisis Costa Rican borrowing quickly reached an unsustainable level; each year from 1981 to 1987 Costa Rican external debt was over 100 percent of GDP.[84]

As the crisis intensified, Costa Rica was repeatedly forced to devalue the colóne. A measure that helped to boost the price of exports, but also fed the problem of the high price of oil and other imports which Costa Ricans relied on for everyday life. The acute structural problems of unfavorable terms of trade, high debt, and a devalued currency also coincided with the inevitable end of the growth cycle predicated on the post-World War II boom, import substitution industriali-zation and the growth that had ensued with inclusion in the CACM. By the mid-1980s, a major structural adjustment of the Costa Rican economy was all but inevitable.

In addition to structural adjustment, an increase in foreign aid provided by the United States also helped to ease some of the strain on the economy. With Costa Rica in dire straits and the U.S.-backed Contras fighting a civil war in neighboring Nicaragua, the United States. provided massive foreign aid to Costa Rica in ex-change for a variety of concessions to help the war effort in Nicaragua. U.S. foreign aid was able to take the place of additional loans, which were becoming less and less available as the Costa Rican government continued to build up debt. The Costa Rican economy's structural problems also put the government under a great deal of pressure to adopt neoliberal reforms based on the Washington Consensus from a number of international organizations. The ultimate solution to the Costa Rican economic crisis of the 1980s depended on large amounts of foreign aid, almost all of it from the United States, deals brokered with the International Monetary Fund (IMF) and World Bank to liberalize the economy, and the political will among Costa Ricans to make radical changes.

An Assessment of Costa Rican Exceptionalism

Given the history of Costa Rica, it becomes apparent that the nineteenth- and early twentieth-century liberal period and the later social democratic model and the values they imbued into Costa Rican politics and society are key to understanding the differences between Costa Rica and the other states of Central America. The liberal period and subsequent social democratic model helped to lay a foundation for more equitable government and economics which smoothed the later transition to neoliberalism. The relative ease with which Costa Rica converted to neoliberalism is in stark contrast to the myriad problems many other developing nations have had in a similar transition. Most importantly, the social democratic model helped to shape the relationship not only among elites but also between elites and non-elites. Post-World War II Costa Rica would never experience the levels of repression present in most of the other states of Central America. In post-civil war Costa Rica "reformist liberalism modernized social relations and triggered the formation of demands for democracy by excluded groups in the twentieth century.[85] At the other end of the spectrum is El Salvador, whose "fourteen families" control over 90 percent of the country's wealth, a factor that underlies the country's civil war of the 1980s.

The key historical factors that differentiate Costa Rica from its neighbors include: spending much of its history as an unimportant backwater, the development of a less unequal distribution of land, and the dissolution of the military. The definitive difference between Costa Rica and its neighbors and the key legacy of the colonial period was the development of a wage labor system and the effect it has had on the way in which different aspects of Costa Rican society relate to one another. The development of a wage labor system also helped in the creation of a unique Costa Rican political culture and underlies Costa Rican exceptionalism, which would save Costa Rica from much of the violence that plagued its neighbors.

While portions of Costa Rica's defining national myth of exceptionalism is questionable, its veracity is largely inconsequential. What is important is that most Costa Ricans believe they are exceptional and act as such. Modern Costa Rica, like any other state, is the sum total of its history and societal level decision making. For Costa Ricans, the idea of Costa Rican exceptionalism, particularly in the time after the Civil War, has informed their decision-making processes. They are exceptional because they believe themselves to be and more often than not make decisions based on preserving this perceived exceptionalism. Costa Rica exceptionalism, therefore, should be seen as a self-fulfilling prophecy conditioned by history. Much of this perceived exceptionalism and the difference between themselves and their neighbors is seen throughout Costa Rican history. From Costa Rican ambivalence to the CAF, to the rivalry between cafetaleros, the subdued radicalism of Manuel Mora, the abolition of the military and the advocacy of regional democracy during both administrations of Óscar Arias, Costa Ricans have thought of themselves as more peaceful and democratic and have used exceptionalism as a motivation to act exceptionally and to create a very different history from its neighbors.

Costa Rican history is also the story of a country that over time was able to build a society-wide consensus on what it means to be Costa Rican and used this consensus to guide its actions. Even with the divergent histories among the states of Central America, it is possible for others to begin the process of change by building a similar society-wide consensus among its people. For Costa Rica, this process took most of its history and similar processes in other countries will also be incremental. However, there are several factors that facilitate the building of societal-wide consensus in Central America that can aid in the development process and the implementation of the Costa Rican model.

The rise of a worldwide environmental ethic and the growth of related NGOs that are willing to assist a country trying to preserve its ecosystem means that an environmental "support system" exists in a way that it never has before. Similarly, the growth and power of international human rights groups helps to spotlight state behaviors that previously would have remained unknown. The most important factor that allows for implementation of the Costa Rican model is the end of the Cold War rivalry and the negative effects it had on conflict throughout the region. The end of the Cold War finally gave the region an opportunity to build a long-lasting peace leading to a much more inclusive democracy. Michael Mandelbaum, in *The Ideas that Conquered the World*, argues for the self-reinforcing nature of peace, free markets and democracy due to the fact that peace leads to free markets, free markets lead to democracy and democracy leads back to peace.[86] In a region that has long suffered the effects of dictatorship and conflict, this opportunity for long-lasting change and empowerment for its citizens cannot be overlooked.

Notes

1. Robert Wesson, *Democracy in Latin America: Promise and Problems* (New York: Praeger, 1982), 75.

2. John A. Booth, *Costa Rica: Quest for Democracy* (Boulder: Westview Press, 1998), 30.

3. Carlos Sandoval-Garcia, *Threatening Others: Nicaraguans and the Formation of National Identities in Costa Rica* (Athens: Ohio University Press, 2004), xiv.

4. Ibid., xv.

5. Ibid., xiii.

6. Catherine M. Marquette, Nicaraguan Migrants in Costa Rica," *Población y Salud en Mesoamerica* 4 (2006): 4-5.

7. T. H. Gindling, "South-South Migration: The Impact of Nicaraguan Immigrants on Earnings, Inequality and Poverty in Costa Rica," *World Development* 37 (2009): 116.

8. Eugenia Rodriguez-Saenz, "Relaciones Ilicitas y Matrimonios Desiguales," in *Politics, Economy, and Society in Bourbon Central America, 1759-1821* ed. Jordana Dym and Christophe Belaubre (Boulder: University Press of Colorado), 188.

9. Bruce M. Wilson, *Costa Rica: Politics, Economics, and Democracy* (Boulder: Lynne Rienner Publishers, 1998), 12.

10. Wendy Kramer, *Encomiendo Politics in Early Colonial Guatemala 1524-154:. Dividing the Spoils.* (Boulder: Westview Press, 1995), 13.

11. Wilson, *Costa Rica: Politics, Economics, and Democracy*, 12.

12. Eugenia Rodriguez-Saenz, "Relaciones Ilicitas y Matrimonios Desiguales," 188.

13. Claudia Quiros, "Hunting Indians," in *The Costa Rica Reader: History, Culture, Politics*, edited by Steven Palmer and Ivan Molina (Durham: Duke University Press, 2004), 20-21.

14. Eugenia Rodriguez-Saenz, "Relaciones Ilicitas y Matrimonios Desiguales," 188.

15. Charles D. Ameringer, *Democracy in Costa Rica,* (Praeger: New York, 1982), 3.

16. Charles Gibson, *Tlaxcala in the Sixteenth Century*, (Stanford: Stanford University Press, 1967), 49.

17. Timothy J. Yeager, "Encomiendo or Slavery? The Spanish Crown's Choice of Labor Organization in Sixteenth-Century Spanish America," *The Journal of Economic History* 55 (1995): 843.

18. Mark A. Burkholder and Lyman L. Johnson, Colonial Latin America, Fifth Edition (New York: Oxford University Press, 2004), 123.

19. Kramer, Encomiendo Politics in Early Colonial Guatemala 1524-1544: Dividing the Spoils, 231.

20. Ibid., 2.

21. Ibid., 13

22. Ibid.,12

23. Ibid., 120.

24. Yeager, "Encomiendo or Slavery? The Spanish Crown's Choice of Labor Organization in Sixteenth-Century Spanish America," 843.

25. Olivier Caporossi, "Adelantados and Encomenderos in Spanish America," in *Constructing Early Modern Empires: Proprietary Ventures in the Atlantic World 1500-1750,* ed. L.H. Roper and B. Van Ruymbeke, (Leiden: Brill, 2007), 61.

26. David J. McCreery, *The Sweat of Their Brow: A History of Work in Latin America* (Armonk: M.E. Sharpe, 2000), 37.

27. William L. Sherman, *Forced Native Labor in Sixteenth-Century Central America* (Lincoln: University of Nebraska Press, 1979), 192.

28. McCreery, *The Sweat of Their Brow: A History of Work in Latin America,* 44.

29. Ibid., 39.

30. Burkholder and Johnson, *Colonial Latin America,* Fifth Edition, 129.

31. Lawrence H. Harrison, *Underdevelopment Is a State of Mind,* (Boston: The Center for International Affairs, Harvard University and University Press of America, 1985), 54.

32. Carlos Monge Alfaro, *Historia de Costa Rica,* (San José: Imprenta Trejos, 1980).

33. Mitchell A. Seligson, *Peasants of Costa Rica and the Development of Agrarian Capitalism* (Madison: University of Wisconsin Press, 1980).

34. Ameringer, *Democracy in Costa Rica.*

35. Harrison, *Underdevelopment is a State of Mind.*

36. Samuel Stone, *La Dinastia de Conquistadores: La Crises del Poder en la Costa Rica Contemporanea* (San José: Editorial Universitaria CentroAmericana).

37. Ameringer, *Democracy in Costa Rica,* 9.

38. Seligson, *Peasants of Costa Rica and the Development of Agrarian Capitalism.*

39. Ibid.

40. Ibid.,13.

41. Ibid., 9.

42. Harrison, *Underdevelopment Is a State of Mind,* 55.

43. Wilson, *Costa Rica: Politics, Economics, and Democracy.*

44. Fabrice Edouard Lehoucq, *Instituciones democraticas y conflictos politicos en Costa Rica,* (Heredia: Editorial UNA, 1998).

45. Booth, *Costa Rica: Quest for Democracy.*

46. Lowell Gudmundson, *Costa Rica Before Coffee: Society and Economy on the Eve of the Export Boom* (Baton Rouge: Louisiana State University Press, 1986), 27.

47. Ibid., 9.

48. Booth, *Costa Rica: Quest for Democracy,* 35.

49. Seligson, *Peasants of Costa Rica and the Development of Agrarian Capitalism,* 3.

50. Booth, *Costa Rica: Quest for Democracy,* 38.

51. Wilson, *Costa Rica: Politics, Economics, and Democracy,* 17.

52. Booth, *Costa Rica: Quest for Democracy,* 19.

53. Consuelo Cruz, "Identity and Persuasion. How nations remember their pasts and make their futures," *World Politics 52* (2000): 298.

54. Cruz, "Identity and Persuasion. How nations remember their pasts and make their futures," 301.

55. Wilson, *Costa Rica: Politics, Economics, and Democracy,* 18.

56. Booth, *Costa Rica: Quest for Democracy,* 36.

57. Jeffrey M. Paige, *Coffee and Power: Revolution and the Rise of Democracy in Central America* (Cambridge: Harvard University Press, 1997), 16-17.

58. John A. Booth, "Democratic Development in Costa Rica," *Democratization 15,* (2008): 721.

59. Booth, *Costa Rica: Quest for Democracy,* 36-37.

60. Paige, *Coffee and Power: Revolution and the Rise of Democracy in Central America.*

61. Deborah J. Yashar, *Demanding Democracy: Reform and Reaction in Costa Rica and Guatemala.* (Stanford: Stanford University Press, 1997), 33.

62. McCreery, *The Sweat of Their Brow: A History of Work in Latin America,* 117.

63. Paige, *Coffee and Power: Revolution and the Rise of Democracy in Central America,* 63.

64. Yashar, *Demanding Democracy: Reform and Reaction in Costa Rica and Guatemala,* 33.

65. Paige, *Coffee and Power: Revolution and the Rise of Democracy in Central America,* 129.

66. Ibid., 8-9.

67. Yashar, *Demanding Democracy: Reform and Reaction in Costa Rica and Guatemala,* 62.

68. Carlos Acevedo, The Historical Background to the Conflict," in *Economic Policy for Building Peace: The Lessons of El Salvador,* ed. James K. Boyce, (Boulder: Lynne Rienner Publishers, 1996), 20.

69. Thomas P. Anderson, *Matanza: The 1932 'Slaughter' That Traumatized a Nation, Shaping US-Salvadoran Relations to This Day. "* (St. Paul: Curbstone Press, 1992), 122-123.

70. Paige, *Coffee and Power: Revolution and the Rise of Democracy in Central America,* 137.

71. Brian Loveman, *The Constitution of Tyranny: Regimes of Exception in Spanish America* (Pittsburgh: University of Pittsburgh Press, 1993), 136.

72. Booth, *Costa Rica: Quest for Democracy,* 48.

73. Mary A. Clark, *Gradual Economic Reform in Latin America: The Costa Rican Experience,* Albany: State University of New York Press, 2001), 23.

74. Thomas E. Skidmore and Peter H. Smith, *Modern Latin America* (New York: Oxford University Press, 2005), 373.

75. Ibid., 372.

76. Clark, *Gradual Economic Reform in Latin America: The Costa Rican Experience,* 40.

77. Booth, *Costa Rica: Quest for Democracy,* 50.

78. Clark, *Gradual Economic Reform in Latin America: The Costa Rican Experience,* 37.

79. Javier A. Reyes and W. Charles Sawyer, *Latin American Economic Development* (London: Routledge, 2011), 146-147.

80. Paige, *Coffee and Power: Revolution and the Rise of Democracy in Central America,* 14.

81. Clark, *Gradual Economic Reform in Latin America: The Costa Rican Experience,* 35.

82. Booth, *Costa Rica: Quest for Democracy,* 157.

83. Ibid., 157.

84. Ibid., 161.

85. James Mahoney, "Radical, Reformist and Aborted Liberalism: Origins of National Regimes in Central America," *Journal of Latin American Studies 33* (2001): 255.

86. Michael Mandelbaum, *The Ideas that Conquered the World: Peace, Democracy, and Free Markets,* (New York: Public Affairs, 2002).

Chapter 3
Ecotourism in Costa Rica

Although Costa Rica's post-World War II economic models would ultimately have to be reworked to include the transition to neoliberalism, the post-World War II era contributed a great deal to the growth of Costa Rica and helped to provide the base from which later ecotourism development was possible, in particular the growth of the Costa Rican middle-class. The growth of the middle-class in the 1950s and 1960s was important for the development of ecotourism because Costa Ricans traveling within their own country were the first wave of ecotourists. With the failure of import-substitution industrialization (ISI), the key event in the post-World War II economic development of Costa Rica was the debt crisis of the 1980s, which combined with a burgeoning environmental movement and rapid deforestation, helped to push Costa Rica to preserve its environmental wealth and consequently to utilize ecotourism as a development strategy. This chapter will examine the development of ecotourism in Costa Rica as a reaction to economic and environmental crisis, after which it experienced long-term growth.

Structural Adjustment, Deforestation, and the Rise of Ecotourism

Similarly to other junctures in Costa Rican history, Costa Rican politicians took the path of moderation when confronted with the need for a major change in policy. Seligson and Martinez Franzoni[1] argue that Costa Rica did not use "shock therapy" and, consequently, economic reform was piecemeal, selective, and embedded within a social-democratic ideology. The transition to a new economic model was also softened by massive amounts of U.S. foreign aid, which helped to supplant foreign borrowing in the short term. The coalescence of several factors gave Costa Rica a unique opportunity to embark upon a new economic model, one that would radically change the face of the country and put it on a path to sustainable economic development. These factors were the economic crisis and subsequent structural adjustment plans, deforestation, the advent of the environmental movement, and the increase in the number of tourists visiting Costa Rica.

Throughout the economic crisis, neoliberalism was implemented through structural adjustment programs spearheaded by the United States Agency for International Development (USAID) aimed at the creation of new sources of export income that would help end Costa Rican reliance on foreign debt, and USAID worked extensively during the crisis with the Costa Rican public and private sectors to create opportunities for foreign investment. At the same time, the Costa Rican government also reached a standby agreement with the IMF in 1982 and World Bank structural adjustment programs in 1985 and 1987.[2]

The goal of these structural adjustment plans was to diversify the economy through the promotion of nontraditional exports in order to boost Costa Rica's foreign exchange. In order to encourage nontraditional exports, one of the major parts of the structural adjustment plan advocated by USAID was a system of tax incentives to encourage growth in a variety of new exports, including textiles, flowers, ornamental plants and foliage, fish, shrimp, and pineapples.[3] Although international lending organizations did not explicitly write a similar plan for the growth of tourism, the Costa Rican government passed the Law of Incentives for Tourism Development in 1985 which provided new incentives to the tourism industry, including "exonerations on import, local, and income taxes to investors in hotels, transportation services (airlines, boats, and rent-a-car services), travel agencies, and restaurant." In addition, the 1985 law set out the following parameters:

Article 1. The Industry of tourism is declared of public usefulness.

Article 2. The present law has the purpose of establishing an accelerated and rational development process of the Costa Rican tourist activity, reason to establish the incentives and benefits to be granted as stimulus for the realization of important programs and projects for such activities.

Article 3. The disposition of the present law will be applied to the following tourist activities:

a) Hotel Services.

b) Air transport of tourists, international and national.

c) Aquatic transport of tourists.

ch) Receptive tourism of travel agencies exclusively dedicated to this activity.

d) Vehicle rentals to foreign and national tourists.

Article 4. The incentives included in this law will be granted by the Costa Rican Tourist Board by way of a tourist contract, prior to approval of the tourism regulating commission, to be named by the Presidency of the Republic. (Article goes on to discuss Bureaucratic structure)

Article 5. For the granting of incentives and benefits stipulated by this law, activities mentioned in the third article, that are currently operating, will be considered as well as new projects and those of enlargement or remodeling.

Article 6. For effects of granting the benefits of this law the following aspects will be taken into account, among others:

a) Contribution on the balance of payments.
b) Utilization of raw material and national supplies.
c) Creation of employment direct or indirect.
ch) Effects on regional development.
d) Modernization of diversification of the national tourist offer.
e) Increase of the internal and international tourist demand.
f) Benefits reflected on other sectors.[4]

The strategy set out in the 1985 law is important because it served as a road map for the future development of ecotourism, and foreign investors quickly began to acknowledge the new reality of the Costa Rican economy. The Organization for Economic Co-Operation and Development (OECD) found that a "significant amount of foreign direct investment flows have been attracted by the tourism industry (while) foreign direct investment inflows into traditional agriculture have tended to diminish."[5] The focus on nontraditional exports paid off when the recovery of the economy in the early 1990s "was led by nontraditional exports, particularly tourism, which by 1993 replaced coffee and bananas as the country's leading earner of foreign exchange."[6] Additionally, in order to broaden foreign direct investment into a larger share of the nontraditional export market, Costa Rica established a system of free trade zones to attract investment into nontraditional exports by offering duty-free imports and a variety of tax exemptions.[7]

The crisis of the 1980s and the structural adjustment policy it spawned were also affected by a parallel crisis, the rapid clearing of Costa Rican virgin rain forest which began on a large scale in the 1950s. While agriculture began losing some of its importance relative to other sectors of the economy starting in the 1950s, it still represented an important sector and much of the strong economic growth experienced by Costa Rica from the 1950s through the 1970s was predicated on the expansion of agricultural exports. Even with attempts at industrialization, during this period "the Costa Rican economy remained an agrarian one. Coffee, the main source of foreign exchange and wealth for some seventy years, remained an important export commodity but slowly lost its top position to cattle and bananas."[8] The increased agricultural production took a very heavy toll on the environment as Costa Rican primary forests were often cleared to make room for the expansion of agriculture and pastureland for cattle and the export of timber. The Costa Rican government also contributed to the problem by encouraging deforestation as a condition of property ownership. Due to this, the Costa Rican economy of the 1950s through 1970s achieved growth while it simultaneously caused very rapid deforestation with the country's percentage of forest cover declining from 90 percent in 1950 to 25 percent in 1990.[9]

This rapid deforestation did not go unnoticed and quickly became a rallying point among environmentalists and was used to focus the efforts of the Costa Rican conservation movement, which pressed the government for solutions:

The voices of many started to become louder for the more rational conservation of natural resources. Lobbying became intensive for the designation of more and more national parks and protected areas. Part of that solution meant that the government would have to take a more active position in legislating protection and funding enforcement.[10]

Due to the role of beef production in deforestation, many environmentalists took specific aim at the cattle industry. Guess argues that the use of a beef quota by the United States, which would provide a steady and reliable income, helped to push much of Costa Rica's agricultural development to cattle farming because bankers were more likely to give credit to safe exports. This resulted in a simultaneous rate of pasture expansion and deforestation during the 1960s.[11] Environmentalists tried to slow Costa Rican deforestation by breaking the link between U.S. beef consumption and Costa Rican cattle farming by organizing a boycott of Costa Rican beef. Their biggest victory was convincing Burger King, who bought one-third of all Costa Rican beef, to stop purchasing it.[12]

By spawning development in ecotourism and manufacturing, Costa Rica's structural adjustment plan had the secondary effect of slowing deforestation because the emergence of the environmental movement and the growth in the number of tourists provided Costa Rica with the opportunity to diversify its economy by capitalizing on money newly available for tourism development which could be used to build ecotourism-related businesses throughout the country. Due to the growth in the environmental movement as a reaction to deforestation and the growth of ecotourism and the revenue it could generate, environmentalism in post-structural adjustment Costa Rica took off. Honey suggests that "propelled by ecotourism, environmentalism has taken root in the national consciousness—just as a tradition of non-militarism had done earlier."[13]

The coalescence of environmental problems and economic crisis would also help to spawn one of the more creative attempts at lowering debt and conserving the environment. This included debt-for-nature swaps which set aside environmentally sensitive land in exchange for relief from a portion of a state's international debt. In a debt-for-nature swap, nations agree to preserve a tract of land as a national park in exchange for having a portion of their foreign debt forgiven. The nation must then agree to use an amount equal to the cancelled debt to help conservation efforts in the new national park. The transaction achieves multiple goals: the preservation of the environment, alleviation of a country's debt, and the likelihood that environmental preservation will continue after the transaction because the money saved is used to help preserve the park. In many ways the best outcome of a debt-for-nature swap is the long-term commitment to reinvest forgiven debts into the park. For instance, Reilly found that "in Costa Rica, interest from debt-for-nature swaps is several times that country's national park budget."[14]

The largest debt-for-nature swap occurred in October 2007 between the United States, Costa Rica and the Nature Conservancy. Using a combination of private and U.S. Treasury funds, Costa Rica had 26 million dollars in debt forgiven with an agreement for that amount to be used toward conservation over the next sixteen years. The areas targeted for preservation are some of the most popular among foreign tourists including the Osa Peninsula, Tortuguero, La Amistad, Maquenque, Zona Norte del Rincón de la Vieja, and the Nicoya Peninsula. With the completion of this deal, the Nature Conservancy states that Costa Rica increased its amount of forest cover back to 52 percent of the country.[15]

The Development of Ecotourism

Until very recently in Costa Rica's history "forest lands were considered worthless on the frontier, and an individual's reputation for hard work depended on the amount of land one cleared."[16] This mind-set, along with the traditional focus on clearing land for agriculture, meant that Costa Ricans had very little interest in conserving the natural environment. Due to this, for most of Costa Rica's history ecotourism was an inconceivable notion. Moreover, the tourism industry in general arrived late in Costa Rica. For instance, Costa Rica did not have its first hotel until 1930 and much of this early development was targeted at Costa Ricans who wanted to spend weekends and vacations at the beach or rain forest since foreign tourists would not begin arriving in Costa Rica in significant numbers until the 1980s.

The construction of the first hotel in 1930 was quickly followed by the passage of Law 91 in June of 1931 that created the National Tourism Board.[17] The National Tourism Board was replaced in 1955 via Law 1917 by the Instituto Costarricense de Turismo (ICT) which was authorized "to promote tourism in general and granted it the power to create national parks, although it never did. Its functions included protecting and promoting historic sites and scenic areas and making tourists feel welcome."[18] Although the benefits of Law 1917 would take a couple decades to be realized, it represented an important step in the development of ecotourism, in particular the central role of the ICT in promoting ecotourism throughout the country.

In the years following World War II, the number of Costa Ricans traveling within their own country would begin to increase, due to rapid economic growth and greater amounts of leisure time. This early development of domestic ecotourism also helped to encourage entrepreneurship among Costa Ricans who were eager to serve this new market. "In the 1960s and 1970s, many tourist resorts, clubs, and parks were developed by Costa Rican entrepreneurs especially for the country's middle and upper classes."[19] Due to the development of ecotourism targeted at a domestic audience, Place[20] found that for much of the 1970s and 1980s the majority of visitors to Costa Rican national parks were Costa Rican citizens. The presence of an early domestic market meant that Costa Rica was able to build up its facilities for ecotourism among its own population before it turned its attention to attracting visitors from abroad. This early growth in a domestic tourism market helped to "prime the pumps" for later development by slowly building the tourism infra-structure.

The majority of foreign travelers to Costa Rica before the 1980s were scientists who were there to study the country's biodiversity. One of the most important was the Organization for Tropical Studies (OTS) which was established in 1963 by six

American universities due to the increased interest in the United States in tropical ecology. In 1968, OTS would greatly expand its presence in Costa Rica by purchasing La Selva biological station in northeastern Costa Rica.[21] By the late 1970s, the number of foreign visitors began to increase, but was still small compared to domestic Costa Rican tourists. For instance, in 1978, 34,000 foreigners visited the national parks, which was less than 10 percent of the total visitation numbers of 357,000.[22]

As ecotourism began to expand, government policy for ecotourism development during the 1970s and 1980s followed two primary tracts: measures to encourage the construction of businesses necessary for ecotourism, such as the Law of Incentives for Tourism Development discussed above, and a range of policies to encourage the formation of a national park system. It is the pursuit of these two areas of development that would assist Costa Rica in becoming one of the prime ecotourism locations in the world.

As Costa Rica attempted to build a profitable ecotourism industry, it increasingly did so through its most attractive ecotourism feature, its renowned national park system. The Costa Rican national park system acts as a showcase for each region's contribution to the country's biodiversity. Costa Rica has been able to take the ruggedness of the land and transform it from an obstacle to be overcome, to a positive developmental attribute. Attempts at conservation in the early days of Costa Rican national park development were necessitated by large-scale deforestation efforts begun in the 1950s.[23]

One of the earliest advocates for Costa Rican conservation was Mario Boza, the first director of the National Parks Department.[24] Boza's motivation for taking the new position was his observation that:

By the early 1970s, Costa Rica was witnessing intensive deforestation to open new lands for agriculture and cattle raising: chaotic land settlement by campesinos (landless peasants), normally following the course of new highways; active trade in wild animal products; very weak environmental education: total indifference to environmental problems on the part of the general public and decision makers; and lack of protected areas that could provide a model of how to conserve nature.[25]

The growth of the environmental movement spearheaded by individuals like Boza played an important role in the formation of Costa Rica's national park system. The key moment in the development of the Costa Rican national park system was the Forestry Law of 1969, which put Costa Rica on a path toward preserving its biodiversity and ecological treasures. Boza would play a key role in advocating for the Forestry Law and predicted that "although from a commercial viewpoint parks might seem like an unnecessary investment, they could become one of the major sources of revenue for the nation."[26] The process that led to the passage of the Forestry Law was also indicative of the growth in the environmental movement because when the law was under consideration "the legislature received an unprecedented outpouring of petitions, letters, and telegrams from various sectors of the country in support of a national conservation policy.[27] Due to its passage, the Forestry Law represents not only the pivotal moment in the creation of the Costa Rican national park system, but also in the Costa Rican environmental movement because it provided environmental preservation with protection under the law. The first park to be protected under the Forestry Law was Cahuita National Monument in September of 1970.[28]

While the development of a national park system was due in large part to the work of activists such as Boza, President Daniel Oduber (1974-78) is widely considered to be the presidential father of the Costa Rican national park system, and his administration ushered in the era of government environmentalism.[29] Especially important for Oduber was the interplay of conservation and tourism as a source of development income, and his administration quickly took to protecting large swaths of Costa Rica as national parks. In many ways, Oduber's vision of the national park system as the backbone of an ecotourism industry was truly visionary, and his administration formalized many of the initiatives of earlier environmental activists. Oduber's administration was "successful in dramatically increasing the size of the Costa Rica park system which did open the door to thousands of *tico* and foreign tourists."[30]

Oduber's leadership was instrumental not only in the formation of the national park system, but also in granting the park bureaucracy a number of powers which greatly increased its autonomy. These changes occurred in the 1977 National Parks Act which made the newly created National Parks Service (SPN) autonomous within the Ministry of Agriculture. The National Park act also established the legal framework for the SPN's work and granted it the power to expropriate land for parks and made it illegal to remove land from park status except by legislative decree. The National Park Act also gave the SPN wide powers to set entrance fees and park regulations, recommend land for new parks, and to run the park system with fewer hierarchical hurdles.[31]

In 1994, the SPN was dissolved and reconstituted as the National System of Conservation Areas (SINAC) which manages and administers Costa Rican protected areas divided into six major categories: national parks, biological reserves, protected zones, forest reserves, wildlife refuges, and wetlands/ mangroves.[32] The creation of SINAC sought to include a wider swath of the Costa Rican people into conservation planning by delegating authority to the regional level by utilizing "the three D's:" deconcentration, decentralization, and democratization.[33] The creation of SINAC was also cognizant of the efforts and desire of Costa Ricans to play a part in the long-term conservation of the land. In 1996, a revision to the Forestry Law would better outline SINAC's responsibilities, which include "conserving forest resources, approving management plans, establishing guidelines for the prohibited use of endangered tree species, and a variety of other administrative functions."[34] SINAC has also been involved in rehabilitating environmentally damaged land. NGOs as well take an active role in protecting landscapes, as they purchase large amounts of degraded land surrounded by remnant forest and promote protecting activities."[35]

In addition to the state-run national parks, Costa Rica has a significant network of private wildlife areas open to the public as ecotourism destinations with approximately 4 percent of protected land privately owned.[36] Because of a 1992 law providing legal designation for private wildlife refuges, owners must develop and adhere to a government approved management plan specifying restrictions on use in order to receive a variety of tax incentives, technical assistance and protection from squatters.[37] The stipulations placed on these private reserves help to provide some protection for areas that could be endangered due to lack of funds and help alleviate some of the pressure on the Costa Rican government to manage every ecologically sensitive area.

These private reserves tend to take one of two approaches to park management. The first approach is to exist in a fashion similar to national park management in which a serious effort is made at conservation and sustainability. An excellent example of this approach is the Monteverde Conservation League which was formed in response to deforestation around Monteverde Cloud Forest. The organization raised money to purchase forested land for conservation. The area they purchased would eventually become "The Children's Rainforest" through contributions from 600 schools in 44 countries.[38]

The second approach to private reserve management is exemplified by another enterprise near Monteverde, called Selvatura Park. The approach here is to provide adventure tourism and to attract as many tourists as possible into the park with little concern about the impact on, and very little dedication to, flora and fauna observation. At Selvatura Park an ecotourist would be hard-pressed to see any animals due to the thousands of people tromping through the area each day while people on zip lines scream above the forest canopy. One can purchase tours of the butterfly gardens, hummingbird garden, and reptile and amphibian exhibition,[39] all of which are essentially tiny zoos rather than any sort of authentic experience integrated into the local environment.

Even with the large amount of public and private land used as parks and nature preserves, it is still very difficult for Costa Ricans to manage all of their natural areas. One problem apparent to many visitors of Costa Rica is the juxtaposition of a well-managed and maintained national park on the one hand, and many areas outside the park system suffering from a myriad of environmental problems, in particular garbage, on the other. It is not unusual to travel from one national park to another and see large mounds of garbage on the side of the road and small streams choked with all types of debris. If managed correctly, private reserves can help to incorporate environmentally sensitive areas into the larger ecotourism picture so they are conserved as well as used to produce income. In addition, while the Costa Rican government has policies in place to expropriate land into the park system, this is often costly and requires the government to seize private assets, something which does not work well within an overall plan of liberalization, in particular attempts to garner foreign investment

The Instituto Costarricense de Turismo

Since its creation in 1955, the ICT has worked tirelessly to develop Costa Rican ecotourism with the mission to "promote a wholesome tourism development, with the purpose of improving Costa Ricans' quality of life, by maintaining a balance between the economic and social boundaries, environmental protection, culture, and facilities."[40] The ICT's functions have changed over time and currently include "strengthening of the processes of formulation and implementation of planning for tourism development, attraction and assessment of investors, development of quality and competitiveness systems, development of marketing in an integral way, tourist attention, generation of information for decision-making, reinforcement of processes for improving administration (comptrollership services, income, administrative analysis, among others."[41] The ICT's current tourism development plan is entitled, Plan General de Desarrollo Sostenible 2002-2010. In this plan, the ICT outlines a number of goals for Costa Rican tourism which focus on three major themes: the need for the economic benefit of ecotourism to be broad-based, sustainable, and family-oriented.[42]

To achieve these goals, the ICT both encourages investment in Costa Rican ecotourism projects and acts as the bureaucratic arm for a number of tourism regulations. One of the ICT's primary regulatory responsibilities is in ecotourism and sustainability certification for the tourist industry, an area in which Costa Rica has established itself as a world leader. One of the oldest and most effective certifications plans is the ICT's Certificación para la Sostenibilidad Turística (CST) which certifies the "degree to which (ecotourism companies) comply with a sustainable model of natural, cultural and social resource management" and does so through a comprehensive checklist of items for both ecotourism agencies and hotels, including the assessment of things such as emissions and the protection of flora and fauna. Inclusion in the program is completely voluntary and open to all types of ecotourism ventures.[43]

The ICT evaluates ecotourism operations in four areas, with each earning a score between one and five leaves:

1. Physical-biological interactions
   Evaluates the interaction between the company and its surrounding natural habitat.
2. Infrastructure and services
   Evaluates the management policies and operational systems within the company and its infrastructure.
3. External clients
   Evaluates management actions taken in its invitation to clients to participate in the company's sustainability policy implementation.
4. Socio-economic environment
   Evaluates the company's interaction with local communities and population in general.[44]

The Costa Rican ecotourism industry takes certification by the ICT very seriously and a high rating is very much sought after. Once an ecotourism business is rated, the CST logo is proudly displayed on its front door. "The CST is widely acknowledged as one of the more convincing attempts to establish visible sustainability credentials within the tourism industry through a system of certification."[45] Costa Rican leadership on ecotourism certification programs is important to the global development of the ability to measure the standards of ecotourism against a defined set of principles. Another important development for the CST came in 2005 when "the International Organization for Standardization established a committee on tourism standardization (and) Costa Rica set up a mirror committee representing all sectors of the tourism industry, as well as government and academia."[46] The result of this was an increase in the number of certified hotels and tour operators as the Costa Rican committee began to pressure the government for more resources to certify ecotourism ventures. This also helped to build a relationship between certified tour operators and certified hotels because the tour operators "announced they would gradually begin to only use certified hotels. Hotels once again began clamoring for certification and recertification."[47]

The linkage between certified tour operators and certified hotels showcases the positive impact that a certification program can have on encouraging the ecotourism industry to adopt environmentally sustainable business practices that are certified by a government agency. The ICT's funding for certification measures has waxed and waned over the years, although recently government commitment to the CST has been on an upswing. The CST is also important because it showcases the commitment to environmental standards across Costa Rica, not just within the national park system.

Another important responsibility of the ICT is to promote Costa Rican ecotourism abroad. One of the most successful ICT initiatives is its "No Artificial Ingredients" marketing campaign. The ICT has done extensive advertising in an attempt to market "No Artificial Ingredients" as the official ecotourism brand of Costa Rica. This brand is successful in part because of the "associated values like democracy, peace, friendliness towards foreigners and conservation as generally accepted norms of society, which together support the sustainable use of its natural resources."[48] The ICT also spends a portion of their budget placing billboards in the airports in San José and Liberia as well as in the United States and Canada including major campaigns in New York and San Francisco featuring "No Artificial Ingredients." The most prominent of these advertisements appeared on a giant screen in New York City's Times Square in December of 2010 where "every two hours for 32 days, a short 15-second promotional video of Costa Rica appeared on the mammoth screen. The ICT estimates that 1.5 million people saw the video, which was projected 1,152 times."[49]

Foreign Direct Investment in Ecotourism

The ICT also manages investment in the ecotourism sector including some projects that are funded through their budget and in cooperation with other parts of the public or private sector. For instance, in 2012 construction will begin on a large convention center, the first to be built in Costa Rica. It is funded through a 20 million dollar investment from the National Bank of Costa Rica (BNCR) and the Bank of Costa Rica (BCR) as well as a 10 million dollar allocation from the ICT's budget. In addition, the Comprehensive Agricultural Marketing Program (PIMA) granted the ICT possession of twenty-five acres of land for the center's construction.[50] Projects such as this are somewhat unusual, given the ICT's main job of coordinating foreign direct investment and promotional activities for Costa Rican ecotourism.

Over the last two decades, Costa Rica has been extremely successful in attracting large amounts of foreign investment in tourism. As the chart below indicates, FDI into tourism from 2006-2010 was quite significant for an economy the size of Costa Rica:

Table 3.1: Foreign Investment in Costa Rican Tourism

Foreign Investment in Costa Rican Tourism	Amount in US Dollars
2006	136, 053, 618
2007	321, 286, 390
2008	291, 519, 976
2009	253, 546, 936
2010 (Q1)	81, 023, 162

Source: ICT, CINDE, Costa Rican Central Bank.[51]

One of the problems inherent in increased FDI into tourism is that much of it tends to be big, foreign-run projects, constructed along the coast, that have more in common with mass tourism in places like Cancún or Jamaica than with traditional Costa Rican ecotourism. Some of these projects also have a questionable commitment to sustainability and the environment. One such investment is the Papagayo project in Guanacaste which, upon completion, was planned to include the construction of 1,144 homes, 6,270 condo-hotel rooms, and 6,584 hotel rooms, a shopping center, and a golf course. Although construction on this project has stalled, it suggests the possibility that the Costa Rican government will begin to move toward grandiose schemes that the local environment will not be able to support.[52]

In many ways FDI in large foreign-owned hotels along the coastline is one of the most problematic aspects of Coast Rican ecotourism. Due to the large amount of investment, pockets of large foreign-owned resorts, many of which "make little claim of being involved in ecotourism"[53] are popping up around Costa Rica, particularly in Guanacaste. The biggest problem with this type of development is that it moves Costa Rican ecotourism away from its core tenets and in all likelihood decreases the amount of money that will be kept in the local economy. As Morales and Pratt point out, there are a number of negative factors associated with the presence of large resorts within ecotourism. With regard to ecotourism development, these new large resorts are:

> associated with greater leakage of tourist spending (smaller contribution per tourist to the local economy), need for greater taxpayer investment in infrastructure (airports, ports, roads, sewer, electricity) and greater expenditures for supporting services (police, fire, medical, etc.). Mass tourism can also potentially lead to congestion and the deterioration of the sites that attracted high value ecotourists in the first place. Similar concerns have evolved from the rise in real estate development in the same coastal areas (referred to by some in the industry as 'residential tourism').[54]

The dominance of foreign interests over Costa Rica's coastline also has a psychological effect on Costa Ricans who see the best parts of their country being sold off to foreigners. By law, all beaches in Costa Rica are publicly accessible; however, this would often require Costa Ricans to brazenly navigate massive resorts past hotel employees who will no doubt try to stop them, thus making this law largely one that is "on paper." Despite myriad laws governing the use and development of its land, particularly in coastal areas, many of these large foreign-owned hotels are in violation of Costa Rican law regarding the environment. For instance, the 1977 Maritime Zone law (Law 6043) dictates that no land within 200 meters of the shoreline may be privately held and nobody can build at all within fifty meters. In order to build outside the fifty-meter barrier, it is necessary to receive a government concession which are typically held for twenty years and overseen by the ICT and the affected local municipality. Foreigners are ineligible for a concession unless they have lived in Costa Rica for at least five years and corporations are ineligible unless half the shares of stock are held by Costa Ricans.[55] Although the Maritime Law sets out to protect the interests of Costa Rican citizens, a large loophole exists in which foreign interests may join in a partnership with Costa Ricans in order to circumvent the law. The combination of large amounts of foreign investment and the need to bypass the law, has led to chaotic and haphazard development. Part of the problem with the development of large coastal resorts is that Costa Rica has become a victim of its own success and has not done a very good job of managing its popularity. This is because, in reality, Costa Rica is no longer seen as an exotic locale that is "off the beaten path," but instead is becoming a common destination for tourists who desire a big resort on the coast.

Part of the problem stems from the reaction to a downturn in tourist arrivals in 2005, which set off a panic in the tourism industry and led to a number of questionable decisions:

Since the Tourism Board (ICT) announced a decrease in tourist arrivals in 2005, a national debate began to identify underlying causes and pay attention to ever-toughening international competition. This has led to a reappraisal of the tourism strategy and increased scrutiny on behalf of NGOs and public institutions. The emerging consensus seems to indicate that an unclear strategy and unmanaged growth could put at risk Costa Rica's niche market for high quality and differentiated tourism services.[56]

The haphazard development of these coastal resorts has not gone unnoticed by Costa Rican conservationists and community groups, many of whom opposed these developments. One of the biggest victories came in 1995 when an Iranian firm sought to build a $50 million "green luxury" resort near Playa Grande on the Pacific coast. Public outcry over the resort's bogus environmental claims caused the project to be shut down and the Costa Rican government made the area a national park.[57] There is also growing evidence that the Costa Rican government might assert itself more fully to manage coastal development. Both foreign and domestic businesses have long ignored the Maritime law by building within the protected beach zone. In recent years, the Costa Rican government, particularly in the last years of the Arias administration, has finally started to enforce the fifty-meter no-build zone, even going so far as to demolish hotels that are in violation of the law.[58]

Despite the pockets of large resorts on the Pacific coast, the majority of ecotourism-related businesses are run and staffed by Costa Ricans. "Outside San José, the capital city, (Costa Rica's) tourism industry has been largely based on small-scale locally owned lodges and hotels which form an integral part of both the communities and natural environments in which they are located.[59] Due to the development of domestic tourism prior to the foreign tourist boom, Costa Rica had a fairly well-developed tourist infrastructure, and many of the small establishments are family-run and operated. In addition, the large resorts are fairly concentrated in a handful of coastal areas, thus leaving the remainder of Costa Rica largely untouched and thus able to remain dedicated to the tenets of ecotourism. The large resorts also tend only to be at the shoreline, with many locally-owned options off the coast. A good example of this is the road leading to Manuel Antonio Park which is dotted with big, foreign-owned hotels with the area directly adjacent to the park made up predominately of locally-owned small hotels and hostels.

The danger to Costa Rican ecotourism is that the country could develop what amounts to a two-track system of tourism composed of big foreign-owned resorts on the coast with questionable environmental records and with very little income remaining in the local community and smaller, locally-owned and authentic ecotourism destinations everywhere else. It is not entirely surprising that some developers opt for projects that increase profits with a comprised set of environmental and sustainability standards. Part of the problem arises from the fact that no matter the plan, there will always be some who do not follow "the vision." For the long-term growth of ecotourism in Costa Rica, it is important that the government have the capacity to regulate ecotourism so that it adheres to principles of sustainability.

Coffee and Ecotourism

The economic crisis of the 1980s also encouraged the Costa Rican government to begin thinking about ways to change the way the coffee industry operated. The downturn of coffee prices in the 1980s would be even more acute than the normal cyclical nature of coffee because much of the downward momentum in the market was spurred by overproduction. This overproduction facilitated the encouragement of a coffee-growing industry in the structural adjustment plans formulated by international lending institutions as a growth strategy for other countries undergoing economic crisis. Interestingly, structural adjustment plans both inside and outside of Costa Rica have had a negative effect on the coffee industry because as the Costa Rican economy moved away from coffee as the World Bank, IMF and others were encouraging coffee production as a source of export revenue in Vietnam, Uganda, and Ethiopia, among many others.

This increased production greatly lowered the price of coffee on the international market and made it difficult for farmers to make a living growing the crop. The International Coffee Organization found that coffee has become more volatile overall since 1989, peaking in 1997, with slightly less volatility since 2000.[60] This overproduction, coupled with the movement of labor and resources to tourism and employment within the industrial sector, caused many Costa Ricans to give up coffee farming. "The collapse of the international coffee market in 1989, coupled with increasing population and land scarcity, have made it difficult for many farming families to continue to rely solely on coffee."[61]

In the last few years, however, coffee has made somewhat of a comeback due to the role of cheap labor from outside Costa Rica and its effect on profitability. As Costa Rican workers have dropped out of the agricultural labor market, the jobs have been filled by immigrants from Nicaragua and Panama who have helped to somewhat stabilize the agricultural sector through their willingness to work for lower wages. "By providing low-wage labor to agriculture, Nicaraguan immigrants have almost certainly helped competitiveness in Costa Rica's agricultural sector."[62]

Costa Rican coffee producers have also benefited from a move toward producing high-quality coffee which often sells at a dollar per pound over market price while also eclipsing the Fair Trade premium. Switching to the production of high-quality varietals was necessitated by the problem of overproduction and the effect that the supply glut played in lowering the price of coffee throughout the 1990s. Since Costa Rica knew it could not compete with countries such as Vietnam which were producing massive quantities of low-quality coffee, they committed to the high-end specialty market and outlawed the farming of low-quality Robusta, in favor of high-quality Arabica varieties. Outlawing Robusta not only helped to focus Costa Rican coffee farmers on a higher-grade product, and thus more profitable exports, it also meshed with the burgeoning environmental ethic in the country since Robusta farming tends to be less environmentally friendly. Danse and Wolters even argue that one of the positive aspects of the coffee crisis for Costa Rican farmers has been "the development of a marketing strategy that is based on economic, ecological and social sustainability and a high end product."[63]

Coffee farmers have also tapped into ecotourism by offering tours of their operations. Among the most famous of these is the Café Britt tour which attracts half a million tourists per year.[64] Not only do the farmers make extra income from the admission price, but approximately 10 percent of those who go on a tour become regular customers of Café Britt's direct marketed coffee.[65] Another way that tourism has boosted the coffee industry is through the increased domestic consumption of coffee by tourists as 90 percent of tourists visiting Costa Rica consume an average of two cups a day.[66]

Since the mid-1980s, ecotourism in Costa Rica has grown tremendously and contributed greatly to the growth of the Costa Rican economy. Ever since Costa Rican farmers began growing coffee they have referred to it as *grano de oro* (gold nuggets); with the rise of ecotourism, Costa Ricans now refer to the money made in ecotourism as *oro verde* (green gold). "This kind of capital influx into Costa Rica, called oro verde, was the hope of people like Luis Fournier, Mario Boza, presidents Daniel Oduber and Rodrigo Carrazo, and others in the conservationist community who saw the potential to make the parks and preserves become self-supporting and assets to the general economy."[67]

Notes

1. Mitchell A. Seligson and Juliana Martinez Franzoni, "Limits to Costa Rican Heterodoxy: What Has Changed in 'Paradise?' in *Democratic Governance in Latin America* eds. Scott Mainwaring and Timothy R. Scully (Stanford: Stanford University Press, 2010).

2. Eva A. Paus, *Foreign Investment, Development, and Globalization: Can Costa Rica become Ireland?* (New York: Palgrave MacMillan, 2005), 140.

3. Mary A. Clark, *Gradual Economic Reform in Latin America: The Costa Rican Experience.* (Albany: State University of New York Press, 2001), 58.

4. Instituto Costarricense de Turismo, accessed March 12, 2012, http://www.visit costa rica. com.

5. Organization for Economic Co-Operation and Development, "Caribbean Rim Investment Initiative Business Environment Report Costa Rica," April 20, 2003, 6.

6. Samuel A. Morley, *Poverty and Inequality in Latin America: The Impact of Adjustment and Recovery in the 1980s* (Baltimore: Johns Hopkins Press, 1995), 185.

7. Paus, *Foreign Investment, Development, and Globalization: Can Costa Rica become Ireland?* 140.

8. Ramon Borges-Mendez, "Sustainable Development and Participatory Practices in Community Forestry: The Case of FUNDECOR in Costa Rica," *Local Environment 13* (2008): 372.

9. Sterling Evans, *The Green Republic: A Conservation History of Costa Rica* (Austin: University of Texas Press, 1999), 40.

10. Ibid., 51-52.

11. George M. Guess, "Pasture Expansion, Forestry, and Development Contradictions: The Case of Costa Rica," *Studies in Comparative International Development 14* (1979): 44.

12. Martha Honey, "Spectrum: Buying Peace with a park – Conservation is not only helping end war in Central America but is also cutting Costa Rica's huge foreign debt," *The Times* (London), February 10, 1988.

13. Martha Honey, "Giving a Grade to Costa Rica's Green Tourism," *NACLA Report on the Americas XXXV* (2003): 41.

14. William K. Reilly, "Debt-for-Nature Swaps: The Time Has Come," *International Environmental Affairs 2* (1990): 136.

15. The Nature Conservancy, accessed October 23, 2010, http://www.nature.org.

16. Charles D. Brockett and Robert K. Gottfried, "State Policies and the Preservation of Forest Cover: Lessons from Contrasting Public-Policy Regimes in Costa Rica," *Latin American Research Review 37* (2002): 13.

17. Instituto Costarricense de Turismo, accessed March 12, 2012, http://www.visitcostarica.com.

18. Evans, *The Green Republic: A Conservation History of Costa Rica,* 219.

19. Martha Honey, Ecotourism and Sustainable Development: Who Owns Paradise? Second Edition (Washington, D.C.: Island Press, 2008), 162

20. Susan E. Place, "The Impact of National Park Development on Tortuguero, Costa Rica," *Journal of Cultural Geography 9,* (1988).

21. Evans, *The Green Republic: A Conservation History of Costa Rica,* 27-28.

22. Ibid., 105.

23. Alonso Ramirez, "Ecological Research and the Costa Rican Park System," *Ecological Applications 14* (2004): 25.

24. Evans, *The Green Republic: A Conservation History of Costa Rica,* 73.

25. Mario A. Boza, "Conservation in Action: Past, Present, and Future of the National Park System of Costa Roca," *Conservation Biology 7* (1993), 240.

26. David Rains Wallace, *The Quetzal and the Macaw: The Story of Costa Rica's National Parks.* (San Francisco: Sierra Club Books, 1992), 15.

27. Evans, *The Green Republic: A Conservation History of Costa Rica,* 68.

28. Ibid., 79.

29. Eduardo Silva, "Sustainable Development and Shortchanging Social Ecology in Costa Rican Forest Policy," *Latin American Politics and Society 45* (2003): 93.

30. Evans, *The Green Republic: A Conservation History of Costa Rica,* 95.

31. Ibid., 102.

32. National System of Conservation Areas, accessed August 4, 2011, http://www.costarica-nationalparks.com/

33. Evans, *The Green Republic: A Conservation History of Costa Rica,* 175-176.

34. Ibid., 179.

35. Jacobus Franciscus Koens, Carol Dieperink and Miriam Miranda, "Ecotourism as Development Strategy: Experiences from Costa Rica," *Environment, Development, and Sustainability 11* (2009): 1232.

36. Ibid., 1232.

37. Jeff Langholz, James Lassoie and John Schelhas, "Incentives for Biological Conservation: Costa Rica's Private Wildlife Refuge Program, *Conservation Biology 14* (2000): 1736.

38. Honey, Ecotourism and Sustainable Development: Who Owns Paradise? Second Edition, 106.

39. Selvatura Park, Accessed July 12, 2011, http://selvatura.com.

40. Instituto Costarricense de Turismo, accessed March 12, 2012, http://www.visitcostarica.com.

41. Ibid.

42. Ibid.

43. Certificación para la Sostenibilidad Turística, accessed June 22, 2010, http://www.turismo-sostenible.co.cr/en/.

44. Instituto Costarricense de Turismo, accessed March 12, 2012, http://www.visit costarica.com.

45. Martin Mowforth and Ian Munt, *Tourism and Sustainability: Development, Globalization, and New Tourism in the Third World,* Third Edition (London: Routledge, 2009), 45.

46. Honey, Ecotourism and Sustainable Development: Who Owns Paradise? Second Edition, 205.

47. Ibid., 205.

48. Luis Morales and Lawrence Pratt, *Analysis of the Daniel Oduber Quiros International Airport, Liberia Costa Rica.* (San José: Center for Responsible Travel, 2010), 10.

49. Adam Williams, "Hotel Closings on Costa Rica's Caribbean Coast spark violence," *The Tico Times,* July 29, 2011.

50. Instituto Costarricense de Turismo, accessed March 12, 2012, http://www.visitcostarica.com.

51. ICT, www.visitcostarica.com, accessed March 12, 2012. CINDE, http://www.cinde.org, accessed March 9, 2011, Costa Rican Central Bank, Departamento de Estadistica Macroeconomica, "Inversion Extranjera Directa en Costa Rica 2007-2008." DEM-048, 22 Febrero, 2008.

52. Mowforth and Munt, *Tourism and Sustainability: Development, Globalization, and New Tourism in the Third World,* Third Edition, 327.

53. Honey, Ecotourism and Sustainable Development: Who Owns Paradise? Second Edition, 165.

54. Morales and Pratt, *Analysis of the Daniel Oduber Quiros International Airport, Liberia, Costa Rica,* 12.

55. Instituto Costarricense de Turismo, accessed March 12, 2012, http://www.visitcostarica.com.

56. Morales and Pratt, *Analysis of the Daniel Oduber Quiros International Airport, Liberia, Costa Rica,* 12.

57. Honey, Ecotourism and Sustainable Development: Who Owns Paradise? Second Edition, 166.

58. Moon Travel Guides, "Costa Rica's Oscar Arias Administration Pulling Down Hotels, accessed August 1, 2011, http://www.moon.com/print/85381. See Also Williams, "Hotel Closings on Costa Rica's Caribbean Coast spark violence."

59. Mowforth and Munt, *Tourism and Sustainability: Development, Globalization, and New Tourism in the Third World,* Third Edition, 326.

60. International Coffee Organization, accessed March 21, 2009, http://www.ico.org.

61. Deborah Sick, "Coping with Crisis: Costa Rican Households and the International Coffee Market," *Ethnology 36* (1997): 271.

62. World Bank, "Costa Rica Country Economic Memorandum: The Challenges for Sustained Growth." Poverty Reduction and Economic Management Sector Unit Report #36180-CR, September 20, 2006.

63. Myrtille Danse and Teun Wolters, "Sustainable Coffee in the Mainstream: The Case of the SUSCOF Consortium in Costa Rica," *Greener Management International 43* (2003): 43.

64. Café Britt, accessed October 14, 2011, http://www.cafebritt.com.

65. Mark Pendergrast, *Uncommon Grounds: The History of Coffee and How It Transformed the World* (New York: Basic Books, 1999), 425.

66. Brenes, Daniel. "Coffee Crisis: Costa Rica Coffee Growers Are Turning to Tourism as World Prices for Brew Sag," *The Ottawa Citizen.* March 17, 2001.

67. Evans, *The Green Republic: A Conservation History of Costa Rica,* 216.

Chapter 4
Ecotourism, Foreign Direct Investment, and the Costa Rican Model

For much of Costa Rica's history, its economy subsisted on the export of agricultural goods, products such as coffee and bananas. While agricultural products are still an important export, their importance relative to other sectors of the economy has diminished. The most striking trend in the Costa Rican economy over the last two decades has been the substantial increases in the level of foreign direct investment and tourist dollars coming into the country and a decrease in the relative importance of agricultural exports and a concurrent decline in agriculture as a percentage of GDP. From 1961 to 2005, the percentage of GDP from agriculture has shrunk from 24.8 percent to 8.7 percent.[1]

The construction of the Costa Rican model in the time after World War II centered on three main debates among policy makers and the Costa Rican people. First, what form should Costa Rican development take? Secondly, how can Costa Rica develop while preserving the environment? Thirdly, what is the best way to solve the economic crisis and install neoliberalism? Not only were each of these questions important, but it was also important that the answer to each question fit together into a coherent plan. In other words, how can Costa Rica develop while protecting the environment through the implementation of neoliberalism?

Superimposed on the development question has long been the appropriate role of agriculture in the economy. Is it central to Costa Rican identity, or do changes in the world economy necessitate a shift to other economic activities? To this day, it is easy to start a debate with a Costa Rican coffee farmer by asking him whether or not the current president is on his side (normally he will argue the president is not). That is not to say that the coffee farmer would be entirely incorrect, as a succession of Costa Rican presidents have tried to increase nontraditional exports at the expense of traditional industries. President José Figueres Ferrer (1994-1998) was instrumental in attracting Intel to Costa Rica based on his belief that "his country would be left behind in its quest for economic development if it remained principally an exporter of bananas and coffee."[2]

The result of the debate over these issues is the current Costa Rican development model which emphasizes ecotourism and foreign direct investment, while maintaining the export of high-value agricultural goods. Costa Rica has been able to develop and modernize by grafting ecotourism onto a model of foreign direct investment, with much of this investment, beginning in the 1990s, coming from companies engaged in high-tech manufacturing. It is this combination of high-tech manufacturing and ecotourism that lies at the center of the Costa Rican model. At the heart of this strategy is the self-reinforcing nature and similarity of the economic policy concerns of both sectors due to the number of junctures in which development policy pertaining to ecotourism and foreign direct investment overlap.

Due to the similarities between ecotourism and foreign direct investment, as Costa Rica embarked on a series of neoliberal adjustments to its economy during the 1990s, there were increases in both the number of tourists as well as the amount of foreign direct investment, with much of this increase at the cost of traditional agricultural exports. The Food and Agriculture Organization of the United Nations found that both the increase in foreign direct investment and "the emergence of tourism contributed to a decline in the relative importance of agriculture in export revenues, furthermore the establishment of Intel as a primary industry in the country, in 1999, led to a substantial decline in the importance of agriculture relative to other sectors."[3]

Coalición Costarricense de Iniciativas para el Desarrollo (CINDE)

The Coalición Costarricense de Iniciativas para el Desarrollo (Costa Rican Investment Promotion Agency), commonly known as CINDE, was created in 1982 at the behest of USAID in the midst of the Costa Rican economic crisis as the lead agency to bring badly needed foreign investment to the country. "Between 1983-1990, the United States contributed $47 million as CINDE's sole source of support."[4] USAID's involvement with CINDE was also due to the Reagan administration's policies in Central America, with particular focus on the civil war in Nicaragua. The Reagan administration hoped that organizations such as CINDE could help to strengthen the private sector and lend stability to the region.[5] Upon its creation, CINDE was charged with the following export promotion–related goal:

1. To contribute to the fundamental civic values that characterize Costa Rica's society, such as liberty, democracy and respect for institutions and laws, justice and peace.
2. Supporting the effective application of the concepts of responsibility and social justice, as important elements within a realistic scheme of national development.

3. To assist in economic and social development for the country's general welfare while strengthening institutions, productive and private entities, and developing exports.
4. Cooperation with the formation of a favorable environment to attract investment for the development of private enterprise.
5. Contribute to the strengthening and restructuring of productive national entities so they can acquire the necessary potential to effectively compete with similar entities in other countries, while improving their knowledge, technology, managerial and technical capacities, efficiency and productivity.[6]

One of the first challenges for CINDE was dealing with the official government entity known as CENPRO (Centro de la Promoción de Exportaciónes y Inversiónes), which was created by law in 1968 as the government-mandated investment promotion agency. Although CINDE and CENPRO would almost immediately come into conflict, CENPRO was not particularly popular in the Costa Rican business community because it was seen as overly bureaucratic. When CINDE was formed, it was specifically created as a private organization whose executive board was, and still is, made up of individuals from the Costa Rican private sector. This attachment to the private sector rather than government gave CINDE an immediate edge over CENPRO. In fact, CINDE was created specifically in order to streamline the process of foreign investment and to avoid government oversight and regulations. It was also able to utilize a great deal of outside expertise and "based itself on a model borrowed from the Irish Development Authority."[7]

With CENPRO jilted, the 1980s saw turf battles between the two organizations until a truce was negotiated in 1989; CINDE would promote investments from abroad and maintain foreign offices while CENPRO would focus on running product fairs and helping small national firms learn how to get into the export business.[8] CINDE was not only tasked with promoting foreign investment in Costa Rica, but to do so through the development of nontraditional exports (anything but bananas and coffee). One of the key features of CINDE is its independence and ability to take the lead on development projects. While CINDE was determined to boost the amount of nontraditional exports, it wanted to do so through the use of high value-added industries. This meant that Costa Rica needed to construct a specific plan for attracting firms that could provide good-paying jobs in industries that were sustainable. In particular, Costa Rica had very little interest in attracting low wage industries such as textiles. In fact, by the mid-1990s, Costa Rica was not particularly attractive to industries that require low-skilled workers at low wages and the ratification of NAFTA in the United States made Costa Rica even less attractive to low-skill/low wage industries that could now place operations in Mexico. Due to the goal of attracting high value-added industries, the strategy had changed, and when firms began to leave Costa Rica for post-NAFTA Mexico, Costa Rica did not try to keep them in-country. As President Figueres declared at the time "we wanted to attract industries with higher value-added, that would allow Costa Ricans to increase their standard of living."[9]

One of the major strengths of Costa Rican policy at this time was the ability to formulate a plan based on a clear consensus on the future of the economy. "The surge of FDI inflows in Costa Rica during the 1990s can be explained in terms of a clearly defined export promotion and diversification strategy . . . based on a clear understanding of the comparative advantages of the country."[10] CINDE's strategy to attract high value-added industry has proved to be highly successful, as the data shows, FDI has grown steadily since 1990.

Table 4.1: Total FDI Inflows for Costa Rica (US$ millions)

Total FDI Inflows for Costa Rica	(US$ millions)
Average 1970s	44
Average 1980s	70
1990	162.5
1991	178.4
1992	226.0
1993	246.7
1994	297.6
1995	336.9
1996	426.9
1997	408.1
1998	613.0
1999	619.4
2000	408.6
2001	460.3
2002	659.3
2003	575.0
2004	793.8
2005	861.0
2006	1,469.0
2007	1,896.0
2008	2,021.0

Source: World Bank[11]

Costa Rica has experienced a significant increase in FDI since 2005 due to the cumulative effect of CINDE's efforts to recruit high value-added industries and the effect that a first major investor within an industry has on other companies looking to invest. For instance, Dell's decision to build a facility in Costa Rica, was due to the success of Intel in Costa Rica, and the World Bank credits Intel with improving the reputation and investment climate in Costa Rica. "As a competitor for FDI, the country can credit Intel with improvement of Costa Rica's image, development of human resources, further insertion of the country in the global economy, and awareness of the country's investment conditions and competitiveness. Intel pushed the country, creating positive pressure to improve, and Costa Rica delivered."[12] The story of CINDE illustrates the way in which an investment promotion agency can lead to real long-term growth when it has a well worked-out plan and follows it. CINDE's success is due in large part for its ability to effectively bridge the gap between government and industry.

Economic Success of the Costa Rican Model of Development

The economic plan put in place as a result of the 1980s debt crisis has been highly successful in diversifying the Costa Rican economy through the encouragement of nontraditional exports. Due to this success, by the early 1990s, ecotourism had passed agriculture as the most important source of foreign exchange. Since that time, ecotourism and high-tech manufacturing have vied for the top spot in export earnings, each easily surpassing the income from agricultural exports. Table 4.2 illustrates the growth in ecotourism and Intel.

Table 4.2: Traditional and Nontraditional Exports in Costa Rica, 2001–2007[13]

Category	2001	2002	2003	2004	2005	2006	2007
Traditional Exports	738.8	691.1	793.8	800.7	758	926.6	10005.5
Coffee	161.8	165.1	193.6	197.6	232.7	227.8	254.9
Bananas	516	477.5	553.1	543.3	481.8	629.5	673.7
Pineapples	133.8	156.2	197.4	255.9	325.7	433.3	485.7
Nontraditional Exports							
Intel	913	927	1401	1208	1444	1785	2075
Tourism	1095.5	1078	1199.4	1358.5	1569.9	1629.3	1894.7

The growth in ecotourism is due to Costa Rica's ability to continually attract tourists, and, as the industry has matured, found strategies to encourage them to stay longer and spend more money, keeping much of it in the local economy. According to Morales and Pratt, Costa Rica's ecotourism strategy:

> has resulted in average tourist expenditures that are well above the international average, accounting for $170 per day and averaging over $800 per visitor per trip. Most importantly, it is estimated that the country keeps much closer to half of the already high value-added earnings from tourism in the local economy.[14]

The growth in high-tech manufacturing and ecotourism has helped Costa Rica to have growth rates that easily outpace others in the region with annualized growth rates from 1990-2005 showing 2.5 percent growth in Costa Rica, 1.9 percent in El Salvador, 0.9 percent in Guatemala, 0.4 percent in Honduras and 0.3 percent in Nicaragua.[15] In addition, ecotourism has a tremendous capacity for continued success with growth estimated at 20 percent a year, nearly six times the industry average.[16]

As ecotourism has become more popular worldwide and countries have begun to use it as a development strategy, there is evidence that it contributes more to economic growth than other sectors of the economy and Brau, Lanza, and Pigliaru[17] found that small economies based on tourism have grown faster than similar economies without tourism. Part of the reason that ecotourism has such a capacity for long-term economic sustainability is due to the propensity for small-scale operations, which help to include local people in the ecotourism industry. The inclusion of local people in the success of ecotourism is important because one of the most significant indicators of the long-term sustainability of ecotourism is its ability to reduce poverty and improve the lives of average Costa Ricans. "The evidence indicates that tourism is contributing to poverty reduction in Costa Rica, with the sustainability approach of the country as a driver of living conditions improvement."[18] Studies have shown that tourism contributes a 3 percent reduction of poverty in Costa Rica and that oftentimes ecotourism destinations such as La Fortuna have higher monthly wages for workers than mass tourism destinations like Tamarindo.[19]

Ecotourism is also sustainable because of its ability to employ segments of the population who often find themselves underemployed, or in some cases unem-ployed, particularly in the developing world. The UNEP found that "(tourism) is among the world's top job creators and allows for quick entry into the workforce for youth, women, and migrant workers . . . in developing countries, sustainable tourism investment can help create job opportunities, especially for poorer sections of the population."[20] Similar to other service sectors, ecotourism tends to be very labor intensive with many jobs not only directly in the industry, but also in related fields. Linkages to other parts of the economy and the subsequent growth in jobs not directly in ecotourism are important for the sustainability of ecotourism because of the effect that ecotourism can have on the overall economy:

> It is estimated that one job in the core tourism industry creates about one and a half additional jobs in the tourism-related economy. There are workers indirectly dependent on each person working in hotels, such as travel-agency staff, guides, taxi and bus drivers, food and beverage suppliers, laundry workers, textile workers, gardeners, shop staff for souvenirs and others, as well as airport employees.[21]

While certainly not perfect, ecotourism is environmentally sustainable because of the need for the conservation of the environment for the use of ecotourism. Over the last two decades, Costa Rica has asserted itself as an international leader in environmentally sensitive policy and was ranked third overall in the 2010 Environmental Performance Index, behind only Iceland and Switzerland.[22] There is also speculation that conservation will continue to be enhanced by ecotourism as increased revenue allows for more land to be preserved as "the increasing trends for nature-based tourism will encourage conservation and tourism revenues (including protected-area fees) to grow in tandem.[23]

While the growth in the number of tourists as well as the amount they spend while in Costa Rica are major factors for ecotourism growth, the key event for the manufacturing sector was the construction of an Intel microprocessor plant in the San José suburb of Alajuela in 1997. The success of Intel has encouraged other high-tech firms to invest in Costa Rica, most notably Hewlett Packard, which has made Costa Rica the fourth largest exporter of high-tech goods and services in the world.[24] No undertaking in Costa Rica's pursuit of high-tech foreign direct investment is more emblematic of the changes sweeping the country than the decision of Intel to build the manufacturing plant in Alajuela. The decision-making process of Intel is also an excellent case study for the reasons behind a large technology corporation's decision to move an important production facility to Costa Rica. In personal interviews with Intel officials, Spar[25] found Intel's decision to build in Costa Rica included many things related to Costa Rican governmental operation and societal values. Reasons included a high level of political and social stability, high quality of life, low levels of corruption, high levels of economic freedom, and relatively high levels of education among the potential workforce

The economic impact of Intel on the Costa Rican economy has been dramatic as the Intel plant alone contributed a 20 percent increase in GDP per capita on average from 1990 to 2005 over the same data with Intel excluded.[26] Intel also helped to set the groundwork for later investment in Costa Rica by other high-tech firms due to the success of the plant in Alajuela and the workforce and educational provisions they negotiated with the Costa Rican government.

Apart from the negotiated benefits, Intel also got a number of unexpected benefits from their partnership with Costa Rica including:

1. A higher level of engineering and software development capacity than expected, which permitted expansion beyond assembly and test into sophisticated services.
2. A high level of managerial maturity, enabling Intel to replace all expatriates in less than two years, rather than in up to three years, the expected time frame for this process.
3. Higher levels of local purchases in goods and services than expected.[27]

The relationship between Intel and Costa Rica has been very advantageous for both sides. Intel got a better workforce than they expected, provided more local employment more quickly, and was better able to integrate into the local economy more than they thought they would.

While Costa Rican growth rate easily outpaces its neighbors, there have been signs of a gradual slowing of economic growth and a measure of economic volatility.[28] For most developing countries, a gradual decline in economic growth is expected given there is less room to grow as they close the gap with the developed world. Creating linkages and reinforcing policy areas in which the needs of the tourism sector and the needs of foreign investors intersect is the key to consolidating the growth of the Costa Rican economy and finishing the process of modernization that arose out of the ashes of the 1980s debt crisis. Particularly important for ecotourism is the minimization of economic leakage by formulating policy that encourages the growth of local businesses so that an ever-increasing portion of profits is kept within Costa Rica.

Attracting Tourists and Business to Costa Rica

Over the last several decades, the Costa Rican government has worked very hard to position Costa Rica as a prime vacation spot and destination for investment from abroad. Both the ICT and CINDE dedicate significant resources to attracting people to Costa Rica. Although the ICT and CINDE's target audiences differ, when examining the literature from each organization, several similarities begin to emerge between the manner in which the ICT attempts to lure tourists to Costa Rica and CINDE lures businesses. Both the ICT and CINDE base Costa Rica's appeal on the following parameters; Costa Rica's peace and stability, educated workforce, the country's proximity to the United States and the ease of travel, ease of financial transactions, and Costa Rica's respect for the environment.

When examining the various tourist brochures produced by the ICT and the businesses promotion literature written by CINDE, each declares the virtues of Costa Rica as a politically and socially stable democracy with no military and a long period of peace. For instance, tourism brochures available from the ICT extol tourists to "explore every corner of this small army-free country; counting more teachers than policemen, a country that lives peacefully and whose major efforts are devoted to improving its health, education and promoting development."[29]

CINDE and the ICT also continually stress human capital issues such as the importance of education in Costa Rica, which has led to an educated Costa Rican populace. Related to this, both CINDE and the ICT stress the high level of training available to its citizens and will often mention, especially with respect to ecotourism, the adherence to "international standards," implying that services available in Costa Rica are to a standard that someone from the developed world would find acceptable. These themes are not only presented as a benefit of Costa Rica in and of themselves, but often both CINDE and the ICT will imply or simply state outright the superiority of these values in Costa Rica when compared to the rest of Latin America. CINDE in particular is acutely aware of sources of competition for foreign direct investment and seeks to position Costa Rica as a safer locale with many benefits of investing there. Both CINDE and the ICT also utilize the absence of the military in Costa Rica as one of the reasons they are able to invest more heavily in human capital than their neighbors.

Both CINDE and the ICT also frequently mention how close Costa Rica is to the United States and how easy it is for Americans to travel there. Both also use the combination of proximity and the uniqueness of Costa Rica as a major selling point for infrastructure issues, chiefly access to modern technological amenities such as cell phone signals, clean water, and utility services All of this is meant to convey Costa Rica's fitness as a destination for both tourist and investment and its dissimilarity to other countries in Latin America.

The primary difference between the way that CINDE presents investment and the ICT discusses tourism is, not surprisingly, that CINDE makes a more business-oriented presentation and the ICT is more concerned about informing potential ecotourists about biodiversity and the possibility of engaging in adventure sports. Due to the ICT's approach, which focuses on the more exciting elements of Costa Rican ecotourism, there is very little mention of anything that could be considered "economic liberalization." While not explicitly stated as such, the ICT's efforts at assuring tourists that Costa Rica is a modern destination that exists as a rustic getaway with modern amenities, helps to put a potential tourist's mind at ease with respect to financial issues, as does Costa Rica's integration into the world economy.

Issues of Regime and the Rule of Law

One of the primary concerns of both tourists and investors is the political and social stability of a destination. This is especially important in a country such as Costa Rica due to the turmoil that engulfed many of its neighbors over the past three decades. One of Costa Rica's basic strengths as a destination for foreign direct investment and tourism is its long history of democratic rule. Costa Rica's long history of democracy has also served to foster a sense of what Chang, Chu and Park call "authoritarian detachment."[30] Often democratization can be reversed not because people do not support democracy, but instead because they have not ceased supporting authoritarianism. Low levels of support for authoritarianism is an indication that democracy is deeply rooted in society and years of democracy in Costa Rica have created a political culture that has almost no attachment to any form of authoritarianism. According to the UN, 94 percent of the Costa Rican population states that they would not support a military government under any circumstance, easily outpacing other Central American states and Latin America in general.[31]

One of the major enabling factors of Costa Rican democracy is the abolishment of the military in 1949 following the Costa Rican civil war. Due to the lack of a military, Costa Rica did not suffer from the problems of civil-military relations and violence that plagued, and continues to plague, many other states of Latin America. For instance, 52 percent of Hondurans and 42 percent of Salvadorans show some level of support for a return to military government.[32] On the other hand, Costa Rica has developed a great deal of cultural pride from the abolishment of the military, and the positive impact goes beyond Costa Rica's ability to spend money it would otherwise spend on the weapons of war on peaceful pursuits; it also means that generations of Costa Ricans have very little experience in the ways of violence. The lack of experience with violence is important because "war spreads guns and the ability to use them. It requires more than technical skill to operate a firearm—it requires psychological readiness, and this mental state spreads quickly in countries afflicted by political violence. In civil wars, few are spared exposure to arms, and the impact of this education lasts a lifetime."[33] Nonviolence and the lack of a military manifests itself by strongly affecting the attitudes of Costa Ricans, and creating a nonviolent, peace-making ethic that permeates Costa Rican society.

Another important issue that flows from political and social stability is the need for personal safety. One way that government policy makers can improve personal safety is by providing an adequate budget for the police and the judicial system. Costa Rica still has some work to do, particularly with respect to the efficiency of the criminal justice system, however it easily outpaces it neighbors in most crime statistics. Recently, Costa Rica has sought to improve its police force and now has 465 police officers per 100, 000 citizens, compared to 326 officers per 100,000 citizens in the United States and has the highest percentage of judges per 100,000 citizens in all of Central America.[34] Costa Rica boosted its police presence in tourist areas in 2006 when the government deployed its first group of 140 tourist police who are charged with assisting international visitors and lowering the number of crimes against tourists. The Tourist Police, who wear white uniforms with "Tourist Police" clearly printed on the back, were deployed to the most popular tourist regions of San José, the Guanacaste beaches, Jacó, Monteverde, Arenal, Los Chiles, and Quepos.[35]

For Costa Rica, decades of democracy and stability has contributed to a political and social system that strongly favors the rule of law. For those wishing to do business, the rule of law with respect to the enforceability of contracts is of the utmost concern. The Costa Rican focus on the rule of law has meant that firms investing in the economy need not fear an impingement on property rights, as Costa Rica has a long history of protecting private property. For many firms that invest abroad, fears of government expropriation of private assets can be a determining factor of whether or not to invest in a given country. These fears are particularly acute in Latin America since many states have a long history of expropriating foreign investment. Biglaiser and DeRouen found that the critical economic reform for foreign direct investment was to minimize the risk of expropriation; a factor they found to be more important than regime type itself.[36] In a region with a history of the expropriation of economic assets by the government, it is not surprising that freedom from government seizure is one of the strongest motivations for businesses to invest. The Costa Rican government has done an excellent job of combining respect for the rule of law with a consistent and coherent economic restructuring plan in which the state has a strong understanding of necessary changes and the best way they can be achieved.

The rule of law and personal security also helps to foster an environment in which human capital is better able to flourish because as the UN argues "development requires security . . . Investors do not put their money in places where the rule of law does not prevail. Skilled labor does not reside in countries where personal safety is at risk."[37] One reason that lack of security and corruption hampers human capital is that it forces job seekers into the informal sector which affects issues from training to worker's rights and taxation:

> Between one-fifth and 40 percent of the economic activity (in Central America) occurs off the books. With the exception of Costa Rica, more than half the employment in Central America comes from the informal sector. These people have opted not to avail themselves of the dispute resolution mechanisms, the labour [sic] protections, or the other benefits of registering businesses and paying taxes. This may make underground firms less competitive, forcing them to accept losses due to breach of contract or default of payment. Informal methods of enforcing agreements or collecting debts may be rooted in violence, representing another source of crime.[38]

Since Costa Rica has been able to build a long-standing and peaceful democracy, they have been better situated to create more human capital, which in turn has positively affected Costa Rica as a destination for foreign direct investment and tourism. Thomas Homer-Dixon argues that technical ingenuity depends on an adequate supply of social ingenuity which is the "key to the creation, reform, and maintenance of public and semipublic goods such as markets, funding agencies, educational and research organizations, and effective government.[39]

Human Capital Issues

While some forms of manufacturing and jobs in ecotourism are low skill, many jobs in high-tech manufacturing and tourism are knowledge-based activities and as such require highly skilled labor. This includes the technical skills necessary to work in microprocessor production or the intimate knowledge of the flora and fauna required by ecotourism. Due to this, one of the primary intersections between the high-tech sector and ecotourism is the need for educated workers. Costa Ricans have come to embrace the knowledge-based economy as an alternative to traditional agricultural development with such a high level of societal consensus that former coordinator of the Council of Presidential Advisors in Costa Rica Andrés Rodríguez-Clare declares that "there is no significant opposition to a development state based on technology and human capital with high-tech multinationals."[40] Uniquely important to both industry and tourism is the need for English language skills since the majority of foreign direct investment and tourists come from the United States.

Table 4.3: Origins of FDI and Tourist by Region

Region	Origin of FDI by percent[41]	Origin of Tourists by percent[42]
USA	62.7%	53.0%
European Union	14.1%	14.0%
South America	4.0%	5.0%
Central America	3.8%	25.0%
Asia	0.2%	–
Other	15.2%	3.0%

Costa Rica has a long history of valuing education among its people, however, prior to the civil war, the literacy rate in Costa Rica was approximately 10 percent.[43] With the abolition of the military, Costa Rica was able to concentrate an immense amount of resources on education, and by 1985, about a quarter of the entire governmental budget went toward education and the literacy rate had topped 90 percent.[44] Currently, Costa Rica has a society-wide literacy rate of 95.8 percent (CINDE) and government-sponsored and required universal elementary education, both of which put the Costa Rican system ahead of most developing world education systems. Costa Rica also has one of the best university systems in Latin America. As CINDE points out:

> The Costa Rican workforce is recognized for its high educational standards and its outstanding productivity level. These capabilities are not only the result of recent efforts, but also the expected consequence of a historical commitment towards the attainment of higher economic growth and improvement of the standards of living, through an energetic and widespread educational policy at all levels of instruction.[45]

The Costa Rican Ministry of Education (MEP) acknowledges the importance of English education and states that "the learner's knowledge of English contributes to the nation's social, economic, and technological development.[46] The MEP confirmed their dedication to the teaching of English as a development strategy in 1997 by mandating the teaching of English in all Costa Rican schools starting in grade one.[47] Furthermore, the MEP takes very seriously early education in English by constructing very rigorous standards. "Costa Rican children are faced with very high stakes around learning to read in first grade, and 15 percent of first-graders are held back for not reading and writing well enough."[48]

The Costa Rican government is also making strides in English education and technical training in post-elementary education, especially for those involved in tourism or working for a high-tech company. In 2009, 13,000 Costa Ricans graduated from conversational English courses with an additional 20,000 enrolled while training a total of 50,000 in its various programs with an operating budget of US$89 million.[49] Taking the lead in this endeavor is the Instituto Nacional de

Aprendizaje (INA) which was created by the Costa Rican government in 1965 to boost the training of Costa Rican workers. "The INA's mission is to promote and develop the vocational training of workers of all sectors of the economy to further economic development and contribute to the improvement of life and work conditions of the Costa Ricans."[50]

With a long-established and solid educational foundation, when Intel wanted to invest, the Costa Rican educational system was in an excellent position to reap massive benefits. As a condition of building the processing facility, Intel required several improvements in education, many of which specifically related to technology and learning English. These requirements included: enhanced curricula at the university level, English reinforcement, establishment of one-year certificates focused on technical fields such as semiconductor manufacturing, and support for technology-related fields. Intel also supported a number of educational projects at the elementary and secondary school levels such as the donation of over a million dollars in computer equipment, the training of teachers in science and technology and programs to raise interest in science.[51]

Costa Rica has long provided an excellent elementary education to its citizens, but has been less successful at the university level in technologically based disciplines and has had many problems in secondary education. The Costa Rican educational system has also had a problem retaining students from the poorest segments of society, who are the students most likely to drop out of school after the elementary grades. When Intel executives were negotiating with the Costa Rican government, they were very concerned that Costa Rican education could not provide the level of expertise they needed in technological production, so many enhancements to the Costa Rican education system were included in the final agreement between Intel and the Costa Rican government, including:

* Programs and enhanced curricula at the three major educational institutions, *Instituto de Tenologico de Costa Rica* (ITCR), University of Costa Rica (UCR), and the Instituto de Aprendizaje(INA).
* English reinforcement at ITCR
* The establishment of a one-year certificate program and a one-year associate degree at ITCR focused on new technical fields such as semiconductor manufacturing and microelectronics, later material science.
* Links to UCR's School of Physics and technological and vocational schools for electronics.
* Support for the electrical, electronics, computing and industrial engineering field.

At the elementary and secondary level:

* The "Intel-Innovation in Education Program, which has donated microprocessors valued at over US$1.1 million to modernize the laboratories in schools.
* Computer teaching programs.
* "Intel-Educate for the Future program, with a goal to train 9,000 primary and middle school teachers in the technological area.

- The "Students as Scientists" program that promotes scientific research in schools.[52]

Due to Intel's continued investments, they have had a very large impact on the Costa Rican educational system. This impact has been enhanced by the Costa Rican government who has embarked on a number of programs to aid in the training of Costa Ricans in many of the skills needed by the labor market, including English for service centers, computer engineering, accounting, and information technology in collaboration with Costa Rican universities, technical schools, and technical high schools.[53] Not only has the Costa Rican educational system integrated instruction in English and technology into education at the elementary, secondary, and post-secondary levels, it also deals extensively with ecological issues in the classroom across grade levels and curricula. For instance:

> Environmental studies are integrated into at least a quarter of the Costa Rican elementary science and social studies textbooks at each grade level, and across the curriculum there is an emphasis on the relationship of the community to its environment. Awareness, care and responsibility for the environment are common recurring themes found from the first through sixth grade science and social studies curricula. There is also a strong focus on the citizen's responsibility to organize, cooperate, and participate at the community level to protect natural resources, plants, animals and all elements of the environment.[54]

Education in environmental science is of great importance for the future of ecotourism in Costa Rica, and many secondary and post-secondary certificate programs have been set up to provide ecotourism relevant education to those who want to work as guides. While in Costa Rica I had the privilege of white water rafting with two young men who were completing their one year certificates to become river guides. When I asked them if they had enjoyed their coursework, they stated "of course, our job will be doing this every day." Costa Ricans have not only embraced environmentalism, but have also embraced the idea of being leaders in ecotourism. As another guide told me later "it's hard to believe my parents gathered palm kernels while I do this for a living."

Proximity and Infrastructure

Another of Costa Rica's strong selling points to U.S. investors and tourists is its proximity to the United States and its very large domestic market. Costa Rica provides a close off-shore destination for foreign direct investment and an easy flight for tourists in search of adventure. One of the key intersections of attracting foreign direct investment and tourism is the quick flight from the United States and the ease of travel once someone is in Costa Rica. Given the passage of the Dominican Republic-Central American Free Trade Agreement, (DR-CAFTA) the proximity of production facilities to the US market will now be coupled with duty-free access to the US market thus further enhancing the significance of location.

While there is nothing that government policy can do to improve Costa Rica's proximity to the United States, there is much they can do to enhance the comparative advantage of proximity by making the trip to Costa Rica more convenient and travel within the country simpler. One of the major problems Costa Rica faces is the inadequacy of its infrastructure. Infrastructure is of immense importance to foreign direct investment and tourism ventures because at the most basic level, high-tech firms and tourist companies share the need to move people and supplies around the country as easily as possible. Given the specific infrastructure needs of tourism, infrastructure development can be driven by tourism. As Blanke and Chiesa of the World Economic Forum point out:

> [tourism] has important indirect positive development effects. It encourages governments to make infrastructure improvements such as better roads, electricity, telephone, and public transportation networks, which, as well as facilitating tourism, improves the economy's overall development prospects and quality of life for its residents.[55]

Currently Costa Rica has two major international airports, San José and Liberia, and thirty regional airports. Costa Rica is in desperate need of more paved roads and two-lane bridges, the lack of which makes some parts of the country, especially on the Caribbean side, very difficult to access. Much of the development of transportation infrastructure has been motivated by making tourism locations more accessible; roads and bridges lead to tourist areas and an incredible array of options for ground transportation are based on the needs of tourists. Currently, the best options for tourist ground transportation are privately-owned companies like the widely used Interbus which provides point to point ground transportation for thousands of tourists a year by picking them up at their hotel and dropping them off at their next hotel. While many of the roads that connect tourist areas are adequate, Costa Rica requires massive improvements and road construction and maintenance outside tourist areas has been somewhat haphazard and underdeveloped. A tourist can spend a day in a van driven by Interbus, going from Manuel Antonio Park to Playa Hermosa in Guanacaste, but when Intel built their production facility in Alajuela, it was necessary for the Ministry of Transportation to take charge of improving the road transportation between the Intel facility and the airport, a distance of less than ten miles. Overall, the worst quality of road infrastructure is found in the Central Valley around the San José area, which is underdeveloped due to a lack of tourist interest, despite producing the country's largest share of exports.[56] The absence of a well-developed system of roads hampers Costa Rica's ability to continue to attract foreign direct investment.

On the other hand, elements of infrastructure dealing with utilities such as phone and electricity, which have largely been driven by agreements with companies that have built facilities in free trade zones, are of much higher quality. Since Costa Rica has worked so diligently to attract foreign direct investment, the quality of the utility infrastructure is much better than the quality of the transportation infrastructure. The World Economic Forum's Global Competiveness Report cites the difference between tourist–driven infrastructure projects and foreign direct investment–driven infrastructure projects very clearly, giving low scores across the board for transportation infrastructure and very respectable scores for electric and telephone.[57]

Over the past several years, electric and cell phone rates from state monopolies have been extremely unpopular and service problems are great topic of conversation among Costa Ricans. These problems do not extend to free trade zones however, because the government reserves lines specifically for companies within this area. This preferential treatment of companies in free trade zones also hampers the development of indigenous company's competitiveness.[58]

The World Bank states that "(Costa Rica's) infrastructure—once the envy of the region—is in need of significant investment and upgrading in order to meet the challenges of a more dynamic and open global economy."[59] When the Costa Rican government began its courtship with Intel in 1995, one of Intel's main concerns was the state of Costa Rica's infrastructure. In order to allay Intel's fears, from 1996-2003 spending on communications and logistics nearly doubled, including the construction of a world-class airport in San José.[60] These improvements in logistics, particularly those involved with the enhancement of infrastructure as it relates to roads and airports are a key factor to attracting business and tourism as both need to be able to move either themselves or their products in and out of the country. Since the improvements made during the push to attract Intel, the government has allowed much of the country's infrastructure to recede. In order for Costa Rica to fully develop its capacity for foreign direct investment and to continue to grow as a tourist destination it is necessary for the government to do a much better job in building a transportation infrastructure outside the tourist trail and a utility infrastructure with fewer problems outside free trade zones. The World Competitiveness Report lists infrastructure problems as the second most problematic factor in doing business next to insufficient government bureaucracy.[61]

Economic Liberalization Issues

While tourists certainly have little concern whether their vacation destination has low tariffs or other specific export-oriented neoliberal economic enhancements, there are many points in which the interests of foreign direct investment and tourists intersect due to the similarities in the desired macroeconomic climate of the place where money is spent. Similar to the desire for political and social stability, tourists and companies engaged in foreign direct investment also desire a location that has experienced a long history of economic stability. The developing world has long been prone to a great deal of economic instability, particularly with respect to the economic policy decisions of its leaders. One of the principal ways that states can benefit from policies that reinforce both foreign direct investment and tourism is by creating and adhering to a coherent development strategy. For approximately two decades, Costa Rica has set out along a path of economic liberalization, reinforced by world institutions that have helped to facilitate the movement toward liberalization by providing funds for a variety of projects. Costa Rica has numerous actors who both facilitate as well as promote Costa Rica's suitability for both foreign direct investment and tourism, such as CINDE and the ICT.

In general, both investors and tourists desire a location that is well integrated into the world economy in order to simplify international monetary transactions. Neither investors nor tourists want to do business in a place that makes international financial transactions difficult and that has not integrated into world financial networks. Any government policy that supports the ease of financial transactions supports the growth of both foreign direct investment and tourism. The specific desires of each sector differs, but the overall operating philosophy of integration and economic openness is important to both. For instance, companies who want to invest in Costa Rica desire economic structures that place no monetary restrictions on receiving, holding, and transferring foreign exchange and that place no restrictions on reinvestment. Each of these desires is emblematic of an economy that is open and integrated. Tourists, though they do not share the specific needs of business, do however benefit from the specificities that flow from an open and integrated economy. An example of this is the desire for the ease of currency transactions facilitated by integrating the banking system of Costa Rica with banks from around the world, thus making the acquisition of currency as simple as bringing your ATM card.

Another principal way in which the preferences of vacation-seeking tourists and profit-seeking investors overlap is the shared desire for value. Costa Rica has become a popular vacation spot as well as investment destination due to their striking collection of attributes for each activity. For the ecotourist, Costa Rica provides an international vacation spot with unparalleled natural wonders at a cost significantly below international travel within the developed world. For most tourists, the single largest expenditure for a vacation to Costa Rica is the airfare, which is normally priced similarly to a long domestic flight within the United States. Due to this, many Americans can travel to Costa Rica at a cost comparable to a domestic vacation. Given the exotic locale, people are able to get a better "bang for their buck," by traveling to Costa Rica. Costa Rica has also been able to position itself in the market as an exotic place with modern amenities, situated within a culturally distinct region, without any of the dangers of a trip to other countries in the region. Companies investing in Costa Rica are also looking for value on the investment. To an investor, this means a skilled, yet inexpensive source of labor, situated in a politically and socially stable country with easy access to the world's largest market.

The ICT has tried to exploit U.S. tourist desire for value by advertising the similarities of the beaches, volcanoes and adventure sports available in Costa Rica to the ones available on a vacation to Hawaii, highlighting the fact that a vacation to Costa Rica would cost a fraction of the cost of a trip to the latter. The depreciation of the dollar versus the British Pound and the Euro has also helped to make Costa Rica more attractive to U.S. tourists. In a May 2008 article Costa Rica is mentioned among the best places to vacation, due in large part to the favorable exchange rate of the dollar to the *colóne*. The article goes on to mention that this is the case because the dollar has appreciated against the *colóne* by about one-third in the last 5 years while also discussing the many tourist sites the country has to offer.[62]

How can Costa Rica create enough value to continue to be attractive to tourists? First, they need to have something that is worth seeing, something which Costa Rica is fortunate to have in excess. Secondly, the things that are worth seeing need to be able to be seen at a price that attracts tourists. State policy can contribute to low prices for tourists by having low taxes, efficient policies against inflation and favorable exchange rates. These measures will help to attract tourists by holding down the costs of a vacation, thus giving a tourist a lot of value for the money. Particularly important for a tourist seeking value is the number of Costa Rican *colónes* their dollars will be able to purchase. Anyone who has traveled abroad is acutely aware of the effect that changes in the exchange rate can have on the enjoyment of a trip and the ability to make one's home currency go farther. A favorable exchange rate is also one of the key macroeconomic policy concerns for exporters. As Clark points out "from (an exporter's) point of view, undervaluation of the exchange rate would be the most favorable policy course."[63]

Environmental Protection

The central issue between ecotourism and industry in Costa Rica is the constraining effect that ecotourism and supporting government policy has on a company's ability to pollute. The profitability of ecotourism gave the natural world a voice and had an important effect on the growth of environmental consciousness and conservation. Costa Rica has become one of the leading producers of high-tech products in the world due to its aggressive pursuit of high-tech firms and has done so while also conserving the natural environment. Much of this success is due to the long-term commitment to environmental preservation that has limited the foreign direct investment coming from firms that would be destructive to the environment. Costa Rica has also spent much of the last half century reversing many policies that encouraged environmental destruction.

Costa Rica has succeeded in the enlargement of its industrial base despite competition from other countries with considerably more lax environmental standards and has often been forced to compete with states that use a corporation's ability to pollute as a comparative advantage. Costa Rica, on the other hand, has concentrated their pursuit of industry to sectors that will not do large-scale harm to the environment due to the importance of their ecotourism industry and the government's continued commitment to environmentalism, including the enshrine-ment in the Costa Rican constitution of the right to a healthy environment and the government's duty to ensure, protect, and preserve that right.[64]

One of the most effective ways to create competition among hotels, travel agencies and tour companies involved in ecotourism is to have a legitimate and rigorous certification process that ecotourists can trust. "The promotion and widespread use of internationally recognized standards for sustainable tourism is necessary to monitor tourism operations and management. The private sector tends to perform best when clear criteria, objectives and targets can be identified and incorporated into their investment plans and business operations."[65] In order for both ecotourism and industry to represent sustainable, long-term paths to development, it is important for both to have rigorous environmental regulation that helps to preserve the environment. In addition, awards given for ecotourism have a positive effect on the implementation of sustainable practices, particularly as there has been a "gradual move toward making eco-awards more rigorous and reputable." (Honey 2008, 66)

Certifications and awards have a strong effect on raising people's consciousness about environmentally sound practices in ecotourism, which is important because ecotourist demand for "green" alternatives is the main driver in their existence. "Tourism market tendencies indicate that the main drivers towards sustainable tourism investment decisions are consumer demand changes."[66] In order for consumer demand to be met with respect for responsible ecotourism, it is necessary for certifications to be rigorous and legitimate. This will allow consumers to award those who engage in real ecotourism.

In 2007 President Óscar Arias created the "Peace with Nature" initiative that lays out Costa Rica's national agenda in pursuit of becoming an international leader in environmental protection and calls on each country to contribute to environmental conservation and to "unite under a new ethic and a new vision of international cooperation that is no longer perceived simply in terms of assistance."[67] In the plan, Arias advocates a long-term national policy with the following elements; a focus on solutions and the implementation of five, ten and twenty year goals with corresponding action plans to accomplish them. He also advocates the search for partners outside the public sector with opportunities for intersectoral, inter-institutional, and citizen participation. This also requires a coherent framework for environmental management through the establishment of follow-up and monitoring mechanisms, including external evaluation. The plan also acknowledges that this will be an evolving process that may require periodic review.[68]

Costa Rica's unique history and the decisions made by its government have contributed significantly to its development and Costa Rica's continued development is contingent upon bolstering factors that reinforce the commitment to both high-tech manufacturing and tourism. The factors discussed in this chapter are vital to Costa Rica remaining on a path toward great economic development. There is still much work to be done to improve the atmosphere of Costa Rica for business and tourism, most notably the need to invest much more money in the infrastructure. However, the Costa Ricans have been very successful in capitalizing on their prior successes.

Notes

1. World Bank, "Costa Rica Country Economic Memorandum: The Challenges for Sustained Growth," (Poverty Reduction and Economic Management Sector Unit Report #36180-CR, September 20, 2006).

2. Roy C. Nelson, *Harnessing Globalization: The Promotion of Nontraditional Foreign Direct Investment in Latin America* (University Park: The Pennsylvania State University Press, 2009), 33.

3. Food and Agricultural Organization of the United Nations, "The WTO Agreement on Agriculture: The Implementation Experience-Developing Country Case Studies." Accessed January 5, 2010, http://www.fao.org/DOCREP/005/Y4632E/y4632e0a.htm#bm10.

4. Mary A. Clark, *Gradual Economic Reform in Latin America: The Costa Rican Experience* (Albany: State University of New York Press, 2001), 57.

5. Ibid.

6. Coalición Costarricense de Iniciativas para el Desarrollo, Accessed March 9, 2011, http://www.cinde.org.

7. Clark, *Gradual Economic Reform in Latin America: The Costa Rican Experience,* 59.

8. Ibid.

9. Nelson, *Harnessing Globalization: The Promotion of Nontraditional Foreign Direct Investment in Latin America,* 34.

10. Organization for Economic Co-Operation and Development. 2003. "Caribbean Rim Investment Initiative Business Environment Report Costa Rica, April 20, 2003.

11. World Bank, "World Bank Economic Indicators" Accessed April 23, 2011. http://data.worldbank.org/data-catalog/world-development-indicators.

12. World Bank, "Costa Rica Country Economic Memorandum: The Challenges for Sustained Growth," 27.

13. Luis Morales and Lawrence Pratt, *Analysis of the Daniel Oduber Quiros International Airport, Liberia Costa Rica.* (San José: Center for Responsible Travel, 2010), 9.

14. Ibid., 10.

15. World Bank, "Costa Rica Country Economic Memorandum: The Challenges for Sustained Growth."

16. United Nations Environmental Programme. "Towards a Green Economy: Pathways to Sustainable Development and Poverty Eradication." Accessed January 5, 2012, www.unep.org/greeneconomy.

17. Rinaldo Brau, Alessandro Lanza and Francesco Pigliaru, "How fast are tourism countries growing? The cross country evidence, in *The Economics of Tourism and Sustainable Development,* eds. Alessandro Lanza, Anil Markandya and Francesco Pigliaru, (Cheltenham: Edward Elger, 2005).

18. United Nations Environmental Programme. 2011. "Towards a Green Economy: Pathways to Sustainable Development and Poverty Eradication."

19. Ibid.

20. Ibid.

21. Ibid.

22. Environmental Performance Index, accessed December 21, 2011, http://epi.yale.edu/.

23. United Nations Environmental Programme. 2011. "Towards a Green Economy: Pathways to Sustainable Development and Poverty Eradication."

24. Coaliciòn Costarricense de Iniciativas para el Desarrollo, Accessed March 9, 2011, http://www.cinde.org.

25. Deborah Spar, "Attracting high technology investment: Intel's Costa Rica Plant," (Washington, D.C.: World Bank Occasional Paper 11, 1998).

26. World Bank, "Costa Rica Country Economic Memorandum: The Challenges for Sustained Growth," 4.

27. World Bank, "The Impact of Intel in Costa Rica: Nine Years after the Decision to Invest." Investing in Development Series, May 2006, 26.

28. Inter-American Development Bank, "Costa Rica: IDB Country Strategy with Costa Rica, 2006-2010," accessed March 15, 2012, http://www.iadb.org.

29. Coaliciòn Costarricense de Iniciativas para el Desarrollo, Accessed March 9, 2011, http://www.cinde.org.

30. Yu-tzung Chang, Yu-Han Chu and Chong-Min Park, "Authoritarian Nostalgia in Asia," in *How People View Democracy,* eds. Larry Diamond and Mark F. Plattner, (Baltimore: The Johns Hopkins Press, 2008).

31. United Nations Office on Drugs and Crime, "Crime and Development in Central America." Accessed March 14, 2012. http://www.unodc.org/pdf/research/central _america_ study.pdf.

32. Ibid.

33. Ibid.

34. Ibid.

35. Overseas Security Advisory Council, "Costa Rica 2010 Crime & Safety Report. Accessed September 1, 2011, http://www.osac.org.

36. Glen Biglaiser and Karl DeRouen Jr., "Economic Reforms and Inflows of Foreign Direct Investment in Latin America. *Latin American Research Review 41* (2006), 69.

37. United Nations Office on Drugs and Crime, "Crime and Development in Central America." Accessed March 14, 2012, http://www.unodc.org/pdf/research/central _america_ study.pdf.

38. Ibid.

39. Thomas Homer Dixon, "The Ingenuity Gap: Can Poor Countries Adapt to Resource Scarcity?" *Population and Development Review 21* (1995), 592.

40. Andres Rodriguez-Clare, "Costa Rica's Development Strategy based on Human Capital and Technology: How it got there, the impact of Intel, and lessons for other countries," *Journal of Human Development 2* (2001), 312.

41. Coaliciòn Costarricense de Iniciativas para el Desarrollo, accessed March 9, 2011, http://www.cinde.org.

42. Instituto Costarricense de Turismo, accessed March 12, 2012, http://www. visit-costarica.com.

43. Stephen Juan, "Costa Rica Invests in Its people; Only Human," *Sydney Morning Herald,* (Australia), August 25, 1988.

44. Vince Magnotta and Ann Magnotta, "Costa Rica's Literacy Boom," *The Christian Science Monitor,* November 4, 1985.

45. Coaliciòn Costarricense de Iniciativas para el Desarrollo, accessed March 9, 2011, http://www.cinde.org.

46. Ministerio de Educacion Publica de la Republica de Costa Rica, *Programas de Ingles III Ciclo,* Accessed December 21, 2008, http://www.mep.go.cr/.

47. Jorge Aguilar-Sanchez, "English in Costa Rica," *World Englishes* 24 (2005), 168.

48. Andrea Rolla San Francisco, Melissa Arias and Renata Villers, "Quality early childhood education in Costa Rica? Policy, practice and outcomes," *Early Years 2* (2005), 116.

49. Coalición Costarricense de Iniciativas para el Desarrollo, accessed March 9, 2011, http://www.cinde.org.

50. Instituto Nacional de Aprendizaje, accessed July 30, 2009, http::// www.ina.ac.cr.

51. World Bank, "The Impact of Intel in Costa Rica: Nine Years after the Decision to Invest." Investing in Development, 22-23.

52. Ibid., 22-23

53. Coalición Costarricense de Iniciativas para el Desarrollo, accessed March 9, 2011, http://www.cinde.org.

54. Steven Lock, "Environmental education for democracy and social justice in Costa Rica," *International Research in Geographical and Environmental Education 18,* (2009), 100-101.

55. Jennifer Blanke and Thea Chiesa, "The Travel & Tourism Competitiveness Report 2007: Furthering the Process of Economic Development," accessed November 5, 2010, http://weforum.org.

56. Eva A. Paus, *Foreign Investment, Development and Globalization: Can Costa Rica become Ireland?* (New York: Palgrave MacMillan, 2005), 161.

57. Klaus Schwab, "The Global Competitiveness Report, 2009-2010," (Geneva: World Economic Forum, 2009).

58. Paus, *Foreign Investment, Development and Globalization: Can Costa Rica become Ireland?* 161.

59. World Bank, "Costa Rica Country Economic Memorandum: The Challenges for Sustained Growth," I.

60. World Bank, "The Impact of Intel in Costa Rica: Nine Years after the Decision to Invest," 17.

61. Schwab, "The Global Competiveness Report, 2009-2010," 120.

62. Sheridan Prasso, "The Best Places to Vacation. (Where the Dollar Is Actually Worth Something)," *Money 37* (2008), 22.

63. Mary A. Clark, "Nontraditional Export Promotion in Costa Rica: Sustaining Export-Led Growth," *Journal of Interamerican Studies and World Affairs* 37, no. 2 (1995): 191.

64. Gabriel A. Quesada, "Garantías Ambientales en la Constitución: Un nuevo modelo ecológico-politico para Costa Rica y el resto del mundo," *Revista de Biologia Tropical 57,* (2009): 472.

65. United Nations Environmental Programme. 2011. "Towards a Green Economy: Pathways to Sustainable Development and Poverty Eradicatio," accessed January 5, 2012, www.unep.org/greeneconomy.

66. Honey, Ecotourism and Sustainable Development: Who Owns Paradise? Second Edition, 106.

67. Oscar Arias, "Peace with Nature." Presidential Initiative: Office of the President of Costa Rica, 2007.

68. Ibid.

Chapter 5
Conclusion:
Lessons from Costa Rica

Although Costa Rica is still part of the developing world, the economic develop-ment it has experienced over the last few decades has made its standard of living well above the regional norm. While there are aspects of Costa Rican history that are exceptional and unlikely to be replicated elsewhere, like the abolition of the military, Costa Rica and the other countries of Central America share a great many things in common such as language, religion, and many aspects of history and culture. It is based on these commonalities that Costa Rica can provide a model for a development path based on the implementation of ecotourism and foreign direct investment. Countries such as Guatemala, El Salvador, and Honduras must, of course, deal with their own histories as they try to build a development plan that constructs long-term peace, stability, and economic development, but they will do so with the example of Costa Rica and the path the nation took to development. In many ways, Costa Rica has become synonymous with ecotourism and is seen as a leader in sustainable development. For instance, Silva argues that "opinion leaders around the world see the nation as a leader and pioneer in community forestry, bioprospecting, 'green' taxes, carbon emissions trading, and administrative decen-tralization in managing protected areas."[1] This chapter will discuss the lessons that can be learned and the steps necessary for the implementation of ecotourism and the attraction of foreign direct investment as a development strategy by using Costa Rica as a model.

Costa Rica as a Model

Costa Rica has earned the reputation as one of the top ecotourism destinations in the world due to its long-term commitment to ecotourism, sustainability and good governance. While other countries have successful ecotourism industries, none has the long-term commitment and viability of ecotourism in Costa Rica. Costa Rica's main strength is the successful implementation of its own development program which has consistently improved the income of Costa Ricans and added to their quality of life. Such a development program did not emerge spontaneously in the minds of Costa Rican policy makers, but rather came to fruition over decades of trial and error. The existence of a long-term plan along with the ability to replicate successful organizations such as the ICT and CINDE, make Costa Rica an excellent example to follow. Not only has the income of the average Costa Rican steadily improved since the 1950s, but a variety of positive lifestyle attributes have helped Costa Ricans to routinely rank among the happiest people in the world including the top spot in the 2010 Happy Planet Index.[2]

Costa Rica represents a usable model because throughout its history, it has had to deal with many of the same external forces that exerted pressure on its neighbors: colonialism, superpower rivalry, and an agro-export economy that existed on the periphery of international economics. Booth, Wade, and Walker argue that Costa Rica developed differently from its neighbors due to the difference in Costa Rica's response to the pressures exerted on it by both internal and external factors: "at key junctures global forces have imposed dramatic alterations in isthmian economies and political arrangements. Local conditions, resources and actors have shaped and channeled these common external pressures to produce divergent local effects."[3] It is the understanding of these "local conditions, resources, and actors" and the way in which their decision-making processes led them to shape and channel outside pressures for divergent local effects that is a key factor in adopting Costa Rica as a model. Another difference between Costa Rica and the other states of Central America is the decision-making processes that also led to the construction of a societal consensus which dictated the way these divergent groups related to one another. Various factors throughout Costa Rican history enabled the inclusion of these groups into the democratic process. Costa Rica's construction of an inclusive democracy is in stark contrast to its neighbors, many of whom have long struggled to create a political system that includes divergent elements of society.

With the end of the US-Soviet rivalry and the civil wars it spawned throughout Central America, it is possible to see the politics of the isthmus beginning to change. Many of the traditional rivalries that have helped to define both Latin America generally and Central America specifically no longer carry the weight they had over the past several centuries. Not only has the cold war rivalry between the United States and the Soviet Union disappeared, the rivalry between the United States and the powers of Europe to create competing spheres of influence in Latin America are at an historic low. For this reason, the end of the cold war has created an atmosphere in which the politics of the region can be completely redone. As John Booth argues:

> The end of the cold war had somewhat reduced the geopolitically driven fear of
> labor and the left that led to determined repression of such forces from the 1950s

through the 1990s. External actors such as the United States, the European Union, the United Nations, and the Organization of American States, now advocate national-level democracy and human rights. Evidence suggests that Central American citizens prefer democracy. There are, therefore many forces that can constrain elites to adopt and maintain democratic rules of the game. This, I believe markedly increases the possibility of successful democratic elite settlements in Central America.[4]

This means that the forces that helped to create vastly divergent politics in Central America are either gone (cold war rivalry) or are at historically low levels (US-European rivalry). This historic change means that the countries of Central America will be able to converge upon a new model of politics and development without high levels of interference from outside powers. The changes over the last few years have helped to create an upsurge in tourism to Central America, and tourists are beginning to discover all the region has to offer. The example of a successful neighbor and the lessons learned along the way, not to mention its missteps, will provide a road map toward a development model based on policies that reinforce ecotourism and foreign direct investment. The availability of a model and regional similarities among the countries of Central America provide the region with an exceptional opportunity not only to develop, but also to integrate. In a study of ecotourism and sustainability projects in Bocas del Toro, Panama, Cusack and Dixon not only argue that one of the advantages for ecotourism development in Bocas del Toro was the successful prototype across the border in Costa Rica, but also point out the possibility integrating ecotourism projects from across the region.[5] It is due to this applicability of the Costa Rican experience coupled with the possibility of change throughout Central America that Costa Rica can provide a development model for the region.

Ecotourism as Comparative Advantage

There are three important factors that help to facilitate the growth of ecotourism: something people wish to visit, the facilities to adequately handle those who want to see it, and an educated populace to make it run efficiently. Underlying these three factors is an adequate infrastructure to move people from place to place with a system of public or private transportation that operates on good roads. Also important are efficient public utilities, particularly sanitation, and a range of accommodations, nightlife and culinary alternatives at varying price levels. Superimposed over these factors is the imperative of economic growth while respecting the tenets of sustainability. When countries have a positive combination of these factors, they can begin to build a comparative advantage in ecotourism over other countries as we have seen in the case of Costa Rica. While much of what Costa Rica has to offer ecotourists is quite distinctive, other countries have their own sets of unique attributes.

Taken as a whole, Central America offers some of the most unique landscapes and cultures in the world: whether it is visiting the indigenous populations in Guatemala, volcanoes in El Salvador, cenotes in the Yucatan, or surfing in Nicaragua, every place has *something*. It is even possible that some destinations have attributes that they do not yet know about because of new discoveries and emerging trends. As Hazbun points out, "new tourism spaces are constantly being developed through the commodification of places, natural geographies, and regionally specific cultural experiences and practices. These efforts to fashion tourism spaces often seek to invent or exploit the rise of new tourism markets and trends such as nature tourism, ecotourism, and heritage tourism."[6]

Due to the singularity of many features of the natural world, countries can have a distinct comparative advantage when they possess attractions that are truly unique. Hazbun argues that the ability of tourism spaces to provide economic benefit "reflects their attractiveness to tourists and tourism firms, their incomparableness, and their international renown."[7] As tourists become more adventurous and less reticent to travel outside the United States and Europe, there is a great deal of room for growth in travel to the developing world. Although the developing world holds a peripheral and often difficult position within the overall global economic structure, tourism is an area in which poor countries can compete with richer ones:

> International tourism is also one of the few trades in which both developed and developing countries can participate more or less on an equal basis, if the right environment is created. This is because while the developed countries may have their Disney Worlds, Hollywoods, historical sites and other sophisticated attractions, many developing countries have areas with distinct and attractive environmental characteristics, such as unspoiled beaches, unique cultural landscapes, natural environments, tropical conditions and other attractions that are not available in the developed world.[8]

The combination of price, exotic location and ecological attributes increases the attractiveness of many locations, and the ease of travel makes them more accessible to a larger number of potential ecotourists. With the expansion of air travel over the last few decades, many Americans can travel in the developing world for less money than traveling to Europe and often less than traveling within the United States. In fact, a trip to many parts of Central America from the eastern United States is faster than a cross-continental flight to the western United States Another important comparative advantage is that given the income structure in the developing world, many countries have a much better ability to create value and thus become an attractive option, a strategy long employed by mass tourism for the marketing of resort vacations. Although it will be more difficult for authentic ecotourism ventures to mimic exceptionally low prices if money is to remain within the local community, the vast majority of developing world–focused ecotourism trips will still have a significant price advantage over international vacations to developed world destinations. In fact, some studies have shown that a tourist's willingness to pay actually exceeds the fee charged for some ecosystems due to their distinctiveness. For instance, over 50 percent of the perceived value of Manuel Antonio Park is not contained in the entrance fee.[9] This means that ecotourists think they are receiving a bargain with places like Manuel Antonio and that there is a high capacity for growth within the ecotourism sector.

Many countries are also able to combine ecotourism with cultural tourism to further enhance the range of options available. Cultural tourism, which is "travel directed toward experiencing local traditions, arts, and heritage while respecting the host community and its surrounding environment,"[10] also contributes to the uniqueness of place and adds to the comparative advantage of a country like Guatemala which has a rich cultural heritage that is largely unfamiliar to people from the United States and Europe. Cultural tourism is an excellent complementary strategy to ecotourism because each places an intrinsic value on an active and exciting experience.

Keitumetse has developed seven strategies to combine ecotourism and cultural tourism:

1. Development of archaeological heritage (archaeo-tourism) in protected areas of wildlife and wilderness value.
2. Recognition of past and present *eco-heritage* (linguistics associated with traditional vegetation, place, and wildlife in the park)
3. Living heritage as illustrated by cultural village activities.
4. Indigenous vegetation use and folklore and folk-life associated with it.
5. Traditional season—animal and vegetation.
6. Recognition of cultural taboos, norms and beliefs associated with animals, plants and protected landscapes.
7. Promotion of local indigenous knowledge systems associated with wildlife and wilderness resources as well as protected areas.[11]

Ecotourism and cultural tourism along with the promotion of local products will also help enhance the attractiveness of a location and will help to keep larger portions of the income within the local population. Traditional culture and locally grown food will lead to a sense of place and authenticity that will help foster respect for the locale. Given the profile of an ecotourist, the more local culture, food and sites that can be incorporated into an ecotourism development plan, the more likely it would be to attract the sort of ecotourist who would contribute to the development of local people.

Due to the attributes that make a locale a desirable destination and the inherent comparative advantage it entails, ecotourism represents a unique opportunity if the necessary elements of society are mobilized to take full advantage of the opportunity. Ecotourism development also requires that all actors in the process make a commitment to the long-term and sustainable development of ecotourism. Williams and Deslandes note the need for many different sectors of society to come together to make ecotourism work and argue that "the economic significance of tourism will need to be taken more seriously. Indeed, there is a greater need today than ever before for policy makers both in government, the private sector and academia to devise policies that will ensure the sustained competitiveness of this very essential industry."[12]

The Role of Democracy in Ecotourism Development

Due to the violent histories of many Central American nations, one of the most difficult challenges to the adoption of the Costa Rican model is the time it will take to build a societal consensus and national identity that facilitates the growth of inclusive democracy in countries that experienced long periods of civil war. Economic development that flows from ecotourism can help to smooth the process and assist in the achievement of some level of societal harmony via the empowerment of local people and their inclusion in decision-making processes. There is evidence that the empowerment intrinsic to community-based ecotourism projects can help to rebuild a society that had long-standing problems. Binns and Nel found that in post-Apartheid South Africa the "potential of tourism-led development to lay a basis for the re-orientation of local economies and to gradually address the Apartheid legacy."[13]

Ecotourism can act as a rallying point for community cooperation and action while ecotourism-driven economic development can act as a means to provide revenue to support the democratization process and the growth of a middle-class. Each of these factors contributes to the evolution of a societal consensus and national identity that helps to create long-lasting peace and stability. The growth of inclusive democracy encompassing values beyond the procedural right to vote, such as individual rights and civil liberties, is an important facet to the construction of a national identity and the development of democracy. John Booth argues that the first lesson that can be learned from the history of Costa Rica is that:

> structural forces lead to democracy. Democratization in Costa Rica did not occur because of the nation's largely mythical equality, homogeneity, and civil traditions. It occurred because structural changes in society undermined the *cafetalero* regime and created new power contenders. Long-term economic change and short-term economic strains created and mobilized working-class and middle-class political forces that eventually gained enough power to win inclusion in the political arena.[14]

With peace and stability there will also be an increase in the rule of law and a decrease in crime and a subsequent increase in feelings of personal safety, all of which help to encourage both the ecotourism industry and dispel the fears of investors that a location may be unsafe. One way to specifically address the safety of tourists is through the development of a tourist police force that is specifically deployed to tourist areas to lessen the number of crimes against tourists and assist them in reporting a crime if they become a victim. The presence of tourist police at popular destinations will help to add a sense of safety and if properly trained, particularly in English language skills, can become an invaluable part of a country's ecotourism portfolio. Tourist police can also be an important expansion of the state's ability to enforce environmental regulations because they will dissuade visitors from engaging in behaviors harmful to the local environment. For instance, the presence of tourist police will motivate visitors do things like stay on trails, resist the temptation to feed the animals and pick up their trash when they leave a park. Although many of these harmful behaviors persist, the Costa Rican government has stepped up efforts in the last few years to increase visitors' awareness of behaviors that can negatively impact a park. For instance, visitors to many Costa Rican national parks are greeted with large signs imploring them not to feed the monkeys because "fed is dead." At Manuel Antonio National Park these warnings are further emphasized with photographs of dead and dissected monkeys—victims of being fed by tourists.

The bigger problem for many states in Central America is improvement in the ability of the police to deal with crime and arrest criminals. Throughout Central America crimes go unpunished at an alarming rate and those who are arrested often do not stand trial for years, if at all. It is very often unsafe to take part in the judicial system whether it is as a victim filing a complaint, as a juror or witness or even as an attorney or judge because of the pervasive violence against those who participate. Apart from the development of a tourist-specific police force, Costa Rica makes clear the benefit of improving the effectiveness of regular uniformed police force and improving the institutional capacity of its judicial system.

The concerns over crime greatly hamper Central America's ability to develop because while for most places around the world the largest constraint on a company's desire to invest is policy uncertainty, macroeconomic instability, and taxation. In Central America, those concerns are secondary to crime and corruption among potential investors.[15] Crime in particular is a clear impediment to ecotourism and frequent stories of violence in a potential vacation spot strongly dissuades potential visitors. In addition, the U.S. Department of State frequently updates travel warnings for U.S. citizens traveling abroad and often includes specific incidents related to American tourists. For instance, this State Department travel warning from September 10, 2010, mentions drug-related violence in Mexico and the potential that Americans could be caught in the crossfire:

> Although narcotics-related crime is a particular concern along Mexico's northern border, violence has occurred throughout the country, including in areas frequented by American tourists. U.S. citizens traveling in Mexico should exercise caution in unfamiliar areas and be aware of their surroundings at all times. Bystanders have been injured or killed in violent attacks in cities across the country, demonstrating the heightened risk of violence in public places. In recent years, dozens of U.S. citizens living in Mexico have been kidnapped and most of these cases remain unsolved.[16]

Despite widespread poverty throughout the region, the two lowest crime rates in Central America come from the richest country in the region (Costa Rica) and the poorest (Nicaragua).[17] While the tie between poverty and crime has long been controversial, many problems for the states of Central America emerge from their lack of democracy and government accountability to the people. Crime, violence, and corruption each play a role in heightening the fears of both tourists and investors and make it less likely they will travel or invest in a country that has widespread problems with crime.

Costa Rican history shows the positive effect of inclusive democracy which not only serves to empower the people, but also to advance an array of positive attributes that will help to move development forward. With a firm development plan in place, states can begin to move forward with the democratization process because of the association between economic growth and democracy, which in turn will contribute to the rule of law. Problems of crime also contribute to one of the major struggles for democratizing states—the need to detach public sentiment from authoritarianism because of its perceived capacity to bring stability through "law and order:

> [Authoritarian regimes'] disregard for human rights is thought to strike fear into the hearts of would-be criminals. Democratic policing, in contrast, appears rather insipid, and police who have operated in both regimes claim that constitutional protections tie their hands. When crime rates appear to increase following national elections, these former authoritarians blame runaway civil liberties and the moral decay of a society of tolerance.[18]

As states democratize, they need to design effective institutions which have the capacity to govern in an effective manner as citizens put more and more demands on government. As Huntington argues, "the development of group consciousness leads the groups to make claims on the political system and to demand participation in the political system. The test of the system is, in some measure, its capacity to respond to these demands."[19] One of the central positive effects of democratization is the increase in the institutional capacity of government which enhances government effectiveness, thus making democracy more attractive and authoritarianism less attractive. The best way to detach citizen sentiment from authoritarianism is to make democracy work, since a functioning democracy will alleviate the fear of disorder and has the potential to empower people so that an authoritarian regime is unthinkable. One of Costa Rica's most notable successes is the preeminence of democracy in the minds of the vast majority of its citizens. Although Costa Rica is exceptional due to the absence of a military, other states can build authoritarian detachment through an institutional structure that adheres to a strict set of rules for civil military relations to ensure the military stays in the barracks. Structurally effective civil military relations will help to give the government a legitimate monopoly on the use of force. One of the biggest deterrents for both tourists and outside investment is a country that is wracked by violence.

Costa Rica demonstrates the positive connection between regime type and the ability to provide services that lead to the growth of human capital, in particular, a well-funded education system. Andres Rodriguez-Clare argues that the first lesson other states can learn from Costa Rica is:

> Costa Rica's long-term commitment to investing in education (which) has been the most important factor behind the recent developments . . . . Countries should not only focus on increasing coverage of primary and secondary education, but should also put in place technical high schools and universities that guarantee a steady stream of technicians and professionals in the areas where the country has a competitive advantage.[20]

One of the key lessons from post-civil war Costa Rica is the payoff of focusing on education over the long-term. Given the mobility and origin of tourists and foreign direct investment in Central America, it is necessary for state policy to focus on English education and training in technology. The extent to which Central American governments can make education a priority will go a long way to determining whether or not they are able to construct enough human capital to aid in their development path.

Start with Ecotourism Development

It is important for states that want to build ecotourism as a development strategy to map out a long-range plan that can be adhered to over time and that protects the natural environment while supporting ecotourism development through the encouragement of local entrepreneurship. The development of multiple sources of foreign exchange across a number of intersectional policy areas that does not rely on a single strategy, whether it is tourism development, agriculture of foreign direct investment is an important asset to the development process. Costa Rica's development path illustrates the importance of ecotourism promotion, the encouragement of foreign direct investment and the continuation of the most important elements (bananas and high-quality coffee) of agricultural model which helped to diversify, stabilize and grow the economy. Paus points out the need for multiple streams of foreign exchange "even with the right proactive policies in place, adopted by a developmentalist state, it is important to see high-tech FDI as only one pillar of development and to use other pillars to address the need for creating jobs, whether that is in tourism, or call centers, or other areas.[21]

Countries can work incrementally toward policies that will allay the fears of investors and tourists alike, but should first concentrate on the development of ecotourism because early in the development plan a country is more likely to attract tourists than it will be to attract foreign direct investment. There are also a number of benefits inherent in the tourism industry that would help to more quickly jump start a country's economy. One of the most important is the ability of ecotourism to create employment due to the labor intensity of the industry and the creation of jobs across a spectrum of skill levels and job types that provide job opportunities across broad segments of society. The economic opportunity of ecotourism will help to empower local people and has the potential to create a positive environment for small-scale entrepreneurship which can provide a base for later, and much larger, economic growth.

The creation of ecotourism-related employment, coupled with the instigation of small-scale entrepreneurship, helps to train locals in ecotourism management which will encourage them to strike out on their own by opening their own tourism-related businesses. In a study of tourism entrepreneurship in South Africa, Nemasetoni and Rogerson found that the majority of those interviewed for the study had prior experience or knowledge of tourism before setting up their own tour-operating enterprises.[22] The trend toward small-scale entrepreneurship can also be seen in Costa Rica where "many middle and lower-middle class Costa Ricans have managed to move into auxiliary businesses associated with ecotourism . . . on balance, ecotourism has brought more income to many Costa Ricans."[23]

The Role of the State

One of the major problems in using ecotourism as a development strategy is that valuable and interesting ecotourism locations tend to be common pool resources, which are often very difficult to manage. Due to this, it is vital that for the state to make environmental protection a priority and ensure that there are mechanisms in place for cooperation between government and the private sector for the enforce-ment of environmental laws and regulations. The state also needs to ensure sustainable ecotourism ventures by making policy based on the idea that, in the long run, preservation will be more profitable than destruction. Focusing a developing state's policies on this principle will certainly be difficult, however, as we have seen in the Costa Rican case, a long-term change in a country's environmental ethic is possible with a combination of citizen activism and appropriate government responsiveness. Furthermore, the Costa Rican case shows that environmental awareness and preservation can be "helped along" through a profitable ecotourism industry. The Costa Rican case also shows that the government can provide assistance by creating government incentives for ecotourism development and foreign direct investment by targeting specific industries within each sector. These incentives should be targeted to parts of the economy and infrastructure that facilitate the expansion of tourism such as improving a country's hotel room and rental car capacity and transportation infrastructure.

It is possible that early in the development of ecotourism the lack of state revenue will require an increase of foreign direct investment in the ecotourism sector in order to jump start development. Although keeping as much money in the local community as possible is the ultimate goal of ecotourism, it might be necessary for some states to initiate their ecotourism plan with a greater degree of foreign investment. Since foreign investors are more likely to build high-end hotels, this investment will contribute to the foundation of a local ecotourism economy, but with room for later development at differentiated price levels that are more likely to come from the local population. While it would be difficult for local people to initiate an ecotourism development strategy, it is much easier for them to find paths of entrepreneurship once tourism is established. Once the market is established, it is much easier for people to build associated businesses and accommodations that keep higher percentages of the income local, many of which are often more affordable than the large corporate hotels that preceded them. The late addition of affordable accommodations would assist in enlarging the market by creating more price differentiation across a spectrum of options. These local establishments along with government policy can also help to minimize the chance of economic leakage.

Since leakage is one of the most important mitigating effects of ecotourism development, it is important for government policy to encourage the use of local products and services whenever possible:

> In destinations where a large percentage of tourist needs are locally supplied (beds and linens, food and beverage, equipment and supplies, labor, tour and transportation services, souvenirs, among others), local contributions and multipliers tend to be high, and the resulting economic impact correspondingly greater. In destinations where substantial income is not captured locally, economic impact from tourism is less.[24]

As tourism has become big business in many parts of the developing world, it is also important for state policy to ensure there is regulation of the tourist trade, particularly important is the certification of sustainable practices in ecotourism-related enterprises. One of the most difficult parts of constructing a certification scheme is developing one that is rigorous and can apply cross-nationally. One such attempt was the formulation of the Mohonk Agreement in November of 2000. In a workshop convened by the Institute for Policy Studies and the Ford Foundation, an agreement was reached regarding a basic framework and certification for sustainability and ecotourism. The framework contains criteria for certification that includes social/cultural, ecological, and economic features and criteria for ecotourism. This framework has helped to establish a number of international certification programs including Green Globe 21, one of the most well-respected sustainability and ecolabel certification programs in the industry.[25] At the national level the ICT's Certification for Sustainable Tourism (CST) has identified Costa Rica as a leader in government certification of sustainability practices. Over the last decade the CST has begun to spread throughout the region. In 2002, tourism ministers from the other Central American countries officially accepted CST as the model to be used throughout the isthmus with some South American countries producing their own certification programs based on the CST model.[26]

It is important that government policy embrace the idea of sustainability and ecotourism certification both to ensure positive outcomes in those areas, but also because successful certification from respected programs will appeal to ecotourists. Mycoo found that "the use of Green Globe 21 certification may well be a marketing strategy, but the environment is benefiting nonetheless."[27] Certification programs can work as a marketing strategy among ecotourists who demand sustainable practices when they vacation and desire to spend money with certified businesses even at an increased cost. Rivera found that room prices for hotels that score high on the CST are positively correlated with higher environmental performance. There is also evidence that indicates a connection between the level of education among corporate leadership and participation in voluntary certification programs.[28] Rivera and De Leon found that "CEOs' level of formal education appears to be significantly associated with higher corporate participation in voluntary programs and also with greater beyond-compliance environmental performance ratings, more so than the more apparent income indicators or country of origin."[29]

Another way in which certification programs and government policy can play a key role in regulating the tourist trade is by making sure that small-scale operations provide an acceptable level of service while operating in a safe manner. In many towns across Central America, many small operations have sprung up in an attempt to profit from the increasing tourist trade by providing transportation, acting as a tour guide, or a combination of many other services. In Antigua, Guatemala, for instance, it seems like every other house has a sign on the door offering to take people to Pacaya Volcano, Copán Honduras, or to give Spanish instruction. Due to the proliferation of small operations, some of them have a less than stellar reputation. For instance, stories of tourists being taken to the top of Pacaya and left there on their own are quite common. In order to allay the fears of incoming visitors, it is important that government policy address these issues if they wish to build a long-range strategy built on ecotourism.

Although it will be difficult for policies to both encourage small-scale operations and make certain that they operate under basic guidelines, it is important that states put in place mechanisms to ensure that ecotourism operations are legitimate. Government licensing, at a nominal cost to the entrepreneur, would be very helpful to establish a basic set of customer service standards. Alternatively basic customer service elements could be introduced into existing ecotourism certification programs. While this is not one of the core social or political concerns of ecotourism, it is an important measure to ensure the long-range viability of ecotourism.

Costa Rica provides an excellent model for government policy related to ecotourism management because of their long experience in the development of an ecotourism industry. This includes both inducements for development as well as regulation and certification of ecotourism-related businesses. In particular, the ICT is a world leader in ecotourism certification programs and provides a long track record of success that other states could emulate.

Ecotourism and Investment Promotion
Integrated into the Global Economy

One of the most important functions of the state for ecotourism development is the need for strict adherence to the rule of law, in particular the enforcement of contracts and the presence of a robust legal and regulatory framework. As Alesina and Giavazzi point out:

> A market economy needs two things in the realm of law and order to function well: first, a judicial system that facilitates transactions of contracts and protects the parties involved, and second, a regulatory environment that achieves the desired goals (ensuring safety, protecting consumers, avoiding negative externalities) without creating unnecessary costs of opening and operating businesses. A key ingredient for the functioning of markets (including financial markets) is the enforceability of contracts, which constitutes the trust that the parties have in the speedy application of the rule of law. A contract is meaningless without a mechanism of enforcement. Developing countries lag behind in the application of the rules of law and contract enforcement, and this is a major obstacle to a fast catch-up with industrial countries.[30]

The rule of law is a key factor in Costa Rica's ability to attract ecotourists and investors and the Costa Rican case illustrates the benefit of a development plan in which the rule of law improves the state's ability to integrate into the world economy. For the last several decades, Costa Rica has consistently formulated policies that have integrated its economy with the larger world, first with respect to agricultural exports and then later for tourism and the promotion of foreign direct investment. As many parts of Latin America are shying away from global economic integration, Costa Rica has embraced it. The most notable example is the signing of the Dominican Republic-Central American Free Trade Agreement (DR-CAFTA) which passed a voter's referendum in October of 2007.

Costa Rica has benefitted from the development of agencies whose mission it is to promote economic development. CINDE's success in promoting investment in Costa Rica emerges from its ability to work well with government while maintaining its own autonomy and a consensus among divergent Costa Rican politicians with respect to their development goals. For instance, "CINDE has benefited not only from its autonomy and transnational learning capacity, but also from the relative ideological consensus among political parties in Costa Rica on working with the business community for the promotion of nontraditional FDI."[31]

It is vitally important that states who wish to encourage foreign direct investment work with or create agencies, government or nongovernmental, that can act as the point organization for large-scale investment. This not only helps to encourage investment, but also coordinates the post-investment atmosphere to encourage further investment, possibly from other companies within the industry.

In Costa Rica, for instance, the success of the Intel plant has helped to encourage investment from an array of high-tech firms.

States that wish to encourage local entrepreneurship near ecotourism areas should also create a legal framework that makes opening a business as simple as possible. The promotion of local entrepreneurship will serve to empower the local population to take a risk and strike out on their own. In order to facilitate these entrepreneurs it is necessary to have a credit system that is accessible for a wide section of the population. This could range from the availability of bank loans for big purchases to the presence of microloan organizations for smaller loans. Any measures that help to empower local people and give them control over their own future will aid in the development process. As Moreno argues, there is a range of positive effects of ecotourism entrepreneurship for local people:

> If enough local people are sufficiently invested in an ecotourism venture and collectively dependent on a CPR (common pool resource) for renewable income, community conservation efforts are more likely to follow. If the community is cooperating in conservation and economic exploitation, their ability to influence the cultural and environmental impacts of visitors will be enhanced.[32]

Another important way to integrate into the global economy is through easing the constraints on traveling in and out of country. In this respect, Costa Rica can serve more as a cautionary tale than as a model since, as anyone who has traveled around Arenal Volcano, or even worse taken the trip to Tortuguero can attest, Costa Rican infrastructure has deteriorated significantly over the last several years from being one of the best in the region to at best the middle of the pack. Modern airports and transportation systems help to facilitate the growth of visitors and investment and, to the extent possible, should be a priority. Although often very difficult for poor countries, the improvement of domestic infrastructure is of the utmost importance to both tourists and those who would like to invest. Due to the difficulty in infrastructure development due to lack of revenue, it is important to initially concentrate infrastructure projects to areas that will create the revenue quickly, so that money can be used to improve infrastructure in other places.

Environmental Consciousness and the Growth of NGOs

The growth of environmental activism in Costa Rica over the last half century is one of the most important elements in the expansion of ecotourism and has acted as both a cause and an effect of environmental preservation. In Costa Rica the post-civil war environmental movement helped to bring about ecotourism through activism related to rapid deforestation and the formation of the national park system which became one of the foundational aspects of Costa Rican ecotourism. As ecotourism has grown, environmental activism has continued to grow as Costa Ricans have observed, and become proud of, their own environmental wealth and the country's worldwide leadership in environmental preservation. This is due to the realization of the intrinsic value of nature and the demonstration of the value of environmental preservation through the lens of ecotourism profitability. Each of these makes a bold statement to developing states about their long-range goals with respect to the environment and the potential profitability of ecotourism as a development strategy. Given the failure of many development strategies and the persistence of poverty throughout the developing world, a new model based upon the example of a country that has transformed itself over the last half decade will provide a fresh perspective with an alternative development path.

One advantage states now have is the existence of a much stronger worldwide awareness of the need for environmental protection and an array of NGOs who are willing to assist. For instance, The Earth Conservancy has been instrumental in facilitating Costa Rica's debt-for-nature swaps while other NGOs have played a significant role in conservation and environmental education:

> What is particularly important for an NGO environmental education center is to act as a change agent in as many respects as possible. The comparative advantage of an NGO environmental education center lies in its grassroots approaches and political independence, which allow it to act more effectively as a change agent. Meeting what is expected by the public from an NGO environmental education center can bring about not only environmental education achievements but also financial self-sufficiency, which is a significant issue for NGO activities in developing countries.[33]

The work of NGOs and the development of civil society will also aid in build-ing the trust necessary for the success of community-wide ecotourism projects, many of which require a great deal of long-term planning. For countries that have a long experience with civil war, the building of civil society is one of its most difficult tasks. Civil society helps to lay the groundwork for projects that are embedded with long-range goals of sustainability because of the need for communities to work together. In a study of La Fortuna, Costa Rica, it was found that sustainable practices are "defined and put in motion by communities with strong community agency, a result of their strong interaction, open communication, participation, distributive justice and tolerance."[34]

In the context of increasing international awareness of environmental issues, the emergence of environmental NGOs and the ability of ecotourism to create revenue, the pace of societal change does not necessarily have to be slow. Luis A. Vivanco perfectly captures the evolution of environmental consciousness that has emerged among Costa Ricans who formerly would not have concerned themselves with issues of environmental conservation when he took a rain forest hike with a local guide:

> On hearing the call of a resplendent quetzal, he hurried ahead to see it. When I caught up to him, he was pointing his camera up a tree at the quetzal and making noises to get its attention. He snapped a photograph, turned to me and announced

"You know, five years ago, I might have shot at this bird with a gun, probably just for the hell of it. But, you see, now I shoot it with my camera.[35]

Achieving Pura Vida para los Todos

The combination of ecotourism and foreign direct investment has changed Costa Rica tremendously in the last half century and there are several lessons that can be drawn from Costa Rica's development path. One of the most important is the potential profitability of environmental protection via ecotourism; due in part to the unique comparative advantage of ecotourism for states with interesting natural features. Due to this, states should pursue a strategy of ecotourism development that lays the groundwork for later foreign direct investment. For states in the developing world, the pursuit of ecotourism can act as intermediary step between an agricultural-based economy and one based upon a combination of ecotourism and industrial development, a step that has been very difficult for most developing countries. The Costa Rican example shows the effects of democracy and supportive government policy in ecotourism development and the construction of environmental awareness throughout society. Each of these factors are key to understanding the success of Costa Rica, as is the role of environmental NGOs. Any policies put in place for ecotourism should contain components that will add to the long-range sustainability of the ecotourism industry and act as a constraining influence on the environmental behavior of industry.

It is also necessary for states who adopt the Costa Rican model to be careful not to fall into a number of possible pitfalls related to ecotourism development. One of the most common is to continually increase prices and thus lose their comparative advantage. Since value for the money represents one of the most important comparative advantages of tourism in the developing world, it is very important that states do not get "carried away" and price themselves out of the market. Although Costa Rica still maintains its comparative advantage in ecotourism, it is possible to discern some movement toward pricing themselves out of the market. Part of this is the nature of tourism and that people will often overspend as they travel. However, part of the problem also stems from the misconception among Costa Ricans that tourists, especially American tourists, have an unlimited supply of cash.

Another important pitfall to avoid is the problem of too many tourists visiting sensitive areas and the potential for ecological damage. Managing economic growth in ecological-sensitive areas will likely prove to be one of the biggest challenges for ecotourism in the future. An especially important issue is the advent of adventure tourism rather than true ecotourism. This not only contributes to the possible destruction of sensitive areas, but also attracts a different kind of person who will interact with the natural environment in a very different way from an ecotourist. If states lose sight of the centrality of the environmental ethic upon which ecotourism is built, it is also much less likely that there will be a positive impact on the local community since adventure packages are much more likely to be booked in advance through foreign-owned companies.

Anyone who has traveled in Costa Rica has heard nearly every Costa Rican they encounter use the phrase, *pura vida*, literally, "pure life." To Costa Ricans, pura vida is a greeting, a farewell, a toast, or simply an exclamation of happiness over life as a *tico* (among its seemingly endless usages). When traveling in other parts of Central America, travelers encounter widespread poverty and very little that could be called *pura vida* in the Costa Rican context. The aim of the Costa Rican model is to spread *pura vida* across the region and improve the lives of the people of Central America, most of whom live in countries that have never been able to break out of the cycle of violence and chronic poverty. These cycles can finally be broken through the empowerment of everyday citizens to take control of their economic future by capitalizing on the ascendency of ecotourism as a development engine. As is evident in the Costa Rican case, ecotourism development can work hand in hand with the promotion of foreign direct investment which will help to diversify the sources of foreign exchange and make long-term macroeconomic stability more likely. In order to do so, it is necessary for states across the region to capitalize on the historic juncture in which the region finds itself and to formulate policies that minimize dependence on agricultural and maximize the benefits of the intersection between ecotourism development and foreign direct investment.

Notes

1. Eduardo Silva, "Sustainable Development and Shortchanging Social Ecology in Costa Rican Forest Policy," *Latin American Politics and Society 45* (2003): 93.

2. Happy Planet Index. Accessed August 21, 2010, www.happyplanet index.org.

3. John A. Booth, Christine J. Wade and Thomas W. Walker, *Understanding Central America: Global Forces, Rebellion, and Change,* (Boulder: Westview Press, 2006), 54.

4. John A. Booth, *Costa Rica: Quest for Democracy,* (Boulder: Westview Press, 1998), 207.

5. Daniela Cusack and Lydia Dixon, "Community-Based Ecotourism and Sustainability: Cases in Bocas del Toro Province, Panama and Talamanca, Costa Rica," *Journal of Sustainable Forestry 22* (2006): 180.

6. Waleed Hazbun, *Beaches, Ruins, and Resorts: The Politics of Tourism in the Arab World,* (Minneapolis: University of Minnesota Press, 2008), xxxv.

7. Ibid., xxxiv.

8. Kwadwo Konadu-Agyemang, "Structural adjustment programmes and the international tourism trade in Ghana: Some socio-spatial implications," *Tourism Geographies 3* (2001), 188.

9. United Nations Environmental Programme. "Towards a Green Economy: Pathways to Sustainable Development and Poverty Eradication." Accessed January 5, 2012, www.unep.org/greeneconomy.

10. S. O. Keitumetse, "The Eco-Tourism of Cultural Heritage Management (ECT-CHM): Linking Heritage and 'Environment' in the Okavango Delta Regions of Botswana," *International Journal of Heritage Studies 15* (2009), 224.

11. Ibid.

12. Densil A. Williams and Derrick Deslandes, "Motivation for Service Sector Foreign Direct Investments in Emerging Economies: Insights from the Tourism Industry in Jamaica," *The Round Table* 97 (2008), 436.

13. Tony Binns and Etienne Nel, "Tourism as a local development strategy in South Africa," *The Geographical Journal 168* (2002), 244.

14. Booth, *Costa Rica: Quest for Democracy*, 207.

15. United Nations Office on Drugs and Crime, "Crime and Development in Central America." Accessed March 14, 2012, http://www.unodc.org/pdf/research/central _america_study.pdf.

16. U.S. Department of State, "Travel Advisory Mexico." Accessed April 23, 2012, http://travel.state.gov/travel/cis_pa_tw/tw/tw_4755.html.

17. United Nations Office on Drugs and Crime, "Crime and Development in Central America."

18. Ibid.

19. Samuel P. Huntington, *Political Order in Changing Societies,* (New Haven: Yale University Press, 1968), 143.

20. Andres Rodriguez-Clare, "Costa Rica's Development Strategy based on Human Capital and Technology: How it got there, the impact of Intel, and lessons for other countries," *Journal of Human Development 2* (2002), 321.

21. Eva A. Paus, *Foreign Investment, Development, and Globalization: Can Costa Rica Become Ireland?* (New York: Palgrave MacMillan, 2005), 205.

22. Irene Nemasetoni and Christian M. Rogerson, "Developing Small Firms in Township Tourism: Emerging Tour Operators in Gauteng, South Africa," *Urban Form 16,* (2005) 22.

23. Martha A. Honey, "Giving a Grade to Costa Rica's Green Tourism," *NACLA Report on the Americas XXXVI* (2003), 44-45.

24. United Nations Environmental Programme. "Towards a Green Economy: Pathways to Sustainable Development and Poverty Eradication."

25. Rain Forest Alliance, Mohonk Agreement: Proposal for an International Certification Program for Sustainable Tourism and Ecotourism, accessed July 7, 2011, http://www.rainforest-alliance.org/tourism/documents/mohonk.pdf.

26. Honey, "Giving a Grade to Costa Rica's Green Tourism," 45.

27. Michelle Mycoo, "Sustainable tourism using regulations, market mechanisms and green certification: A case study of Barbados," *Journal of Sustainable Tourism 14* (2006), 505.

28. Jorge Rivera, "Assessing a Voluntary environmental initiative in the developing world: The Costa Rican Certification for Sustainable Tourism," *Policy Studies 35,* (2002).

29. Jorge Rivera and Peter De Leon, "Chief Executive Officers and voluntary environmental performance: Costa Rica's certification for sustainable tourism," *Policy Sciences 38* (2005), 122.

30. Alberto Alesina and Francesco Giavazzi, *The Future of Europe: Reform of Decline.* (Boston: MIT Press, 2008), 101.

31. Roy C. Nelson, "Competing for Foreign Direct Investment: Efforts to Promote Nontraditional FDI in Costa Rica, Brazil, and Chile," *Studies in Comparative International Development 40* (2005), 16.

32. Peter S. Moreno, "Ecotourism Along the Meso-American Caribbean Reef: The Impacts of Foreign Investment," *Human Ecology 33* (2005): 242.

33.   Ko Nomura, Latipah Hendarti and Osamu Abe, "NGO Environmental Education Centers in Developing Countries: Role, Significance, and Keys to Success, from a 'Change Agent' Perspective," *International Review for Environmental Strategies 4* (2003), 181.

34.   David Matarrita-Cascante, Mark Anthony Brennan and A. E. Luloff, "Community Agency and Sustainable Tourism Development: The Case of La Fortuna, Costa Rica," *Journal of Sustainable Tourism 18* (2010), 749.

35.   Luis A. Vivanco, "Spectacular Quetzals, Ecotourism, and Environmental Futures in Monte Verde, Costa Rica," *Ethnology 40* (2001), 79-80.

Bibliography

Acevedo, Carlos. "The Historical Background to the Conflict." Pp. 19-30 in *Economic Policy for Building Peace: The Lessons of El Salvador,* edited by James K. Boyce. Boulder: Lynne Rienner Publishers, 1996.

Aguilar-Sanchez. "English in Costa Rica." *World Englishes* 24 (2005): 161-72.

Akama, J. S. and Kieti, D. M. "Tourism and Socio-economic Development in Developing Countries: A Case Study of Mombasa Resort in Kenya." *Journal of Sustainable Tourism* 15 (2007): 735-48.

Alesina, Alberto and Francesco Giavazzi. *The Future of Europe: Reform of Decline.* Boston: MIT Press, 2008.

Ameringer, Charles D. *Democracy in Costa Rica.* New York: Praegar, 1982.

Andereck, Kathleen L., "Tourists' perceptions of environmentally responsible innovations at tourism businesses." *Journal of Sustainable Tourism* 17 (2009): 489-99

Anderson, Thomas P. *Matanza: The 1932 "Slaughter" That Traumatized a Nation, Shaping US-Salvadoran Relations to This Day.* St. Paul: Curbstone Press, 1992.

Arias, Oscar. "Peace, Development, and the Environment: Challenges to the Costa Rican Model." Barnard Environmental Lecture, American Association for the Advancement of Science: Washington, D.C., September 7, 2004.

———. "Peace with Nature." Presidential Initiative: Office of the President of Costa Rica, 2007.

Banco Central de Costa Rica Departamento de Estadistica Macroeconomica. "Inversion Extranjera Directa en Costa Rica 2007-2008." DEM-048, 22 Febrero, 2008.

Bhatt, Seema and Syed Liyakhat. *Ecotourism Development in India: Communities, Capital and Conservation.* New Delhi: Cambridge University Press India Pvt. Ltd., 2008.

Biglaiser, Glen and Karl DeRouen Jr. "Economic Reforms and Inflows of Foreign Direct Investment in Latin America." *Latin American Research* Review 41 (2006): 51-75.

Binns, Tony and Etienne Nel. "Tourism as a local development strategy in South Africa." *The Geographical Journal* 168 (2002): 235-247.

Blanke, Jennifer and Thea Chiesa. *The Travel & Tourism Competitiveness Report 2007: Furthering the Process of Economic Development* (Geneva: World Economic Forum, 2007) Accessed November 5, 2010, http:// weforum.org.

Booth, John A. *Costa Rica: Quest for Democracy.* Boulder: Westview Press, 1998.

———. "Democratic Development in Costa Rica." *Democratization 15* (2008): 714-32.

————, Christine J. Wade and Thomas W. Walker, *Understanding Central America: Global Forces, Rebellion, and Change*. Boulder: Westview Press, 2006.

Borges-Mendez, Ramon. "Sustainable Development and Participatory Practices in Community Forestry: The Case of FUNDECOR in Costa Rica." *Local Environment 13* (2008): 367-83.

Boza, Mario A. "Conservation in Action: Past, Present, and Future of the National Park System of Costa Rica." *Conservation Biology 7* (1993): 239-47.

Brau, Rinaldo, Alessandro Lanza and Francesco Pigliaru. "How fast are tourism countries growing? The cross country evidence." Pp. 8-29 in *The Economics of Tourism and Sustainable Development,* edited by Alessandro Lanza, Anil Markandya and Francesco Pigliaru. Cheltenham: Edward Elger, 2005.

Brenes, Daniel. "Coffee Crisis: Costa Rica Coffee Growers Are Turning to Tourism as World Prices for Brew Sag." *The Ottawa Citizen.* March 17, 2001.

Brockett, Charles D. and Robert K. Gottfried. "State Policies and the Preservation of Forest Cover: Lessons from Contrasting Public-Policy Regimes in Costa Rica." *Latin American Research Review 37* (2002): 7-40.

Burkholder, Mark A. and Lyman L. Johnson. *Colonial Latin America*, Fifth Edition. New York: Oxford University Press, 2004.

Café Britt. accessed October 14, 2011, http://www.cafebritt.com

Caporossi, Olivier. "Adelantados and Encomenderos in Spanish America." Pp. 55-78 in *Constructing Early Modern Empires: Proprietary Ventures in the Atlantic World 1500-1750,* edited by L.H. Roper and B. Van Ruymbeke. Leiden: Brill, 2007

Caribbean Tourism Organization. "A rough ride for luxury travel." Accessed October 10, 2010, http://www.onecaribbean.

Ceballas-Lascurain, Hector. "The Future of Ecotourism." *Mexico Journal 1* (1987): 13-14.

Certificación para la Sostenibilidad Turística, accessed June 22, 2010, http://www.turismo-sostenible.co.cr/en/.

Chan, Jennifer Lian Kim and Tom Baum. "Ecotourists' Perception of Ecotourism Experience in Lower Kinabatangan, Sabah, Malaysia." *Journal of Sustainable Tourism 15* (2007): 574-90.

Chang, Yu-tzung, Yu-Han Chu, and Chong-Min Park. "Authoritarian Nostalgia in Asia." Pp. 74-88 in *How People View Democracy,* edited by Larry Diamond and Marc F. Plattner. Baltimore: The Johns Hopkins Press, 2008.

Chase, Lisa C., David R. Lee, William D. Schulze, and Deborah J. Anderson. "Ecotourism Demand and Differential Pricing of National Park Access in Costa Rica." *Land Economics 74* (1998): 466-82.

Clapp, Jennifer. "Food Price Volatility in the Global South: Considering the Global Economic Context." *Third World Quarterly 30* (2009): 1183-96.

Clark, Mary A. "Nontraditional Export Promotion in Costa Rica: Sustaining Export-Led Growth." *Journal of Interamerican Studies and World Affairs 37* (1995): 181-223.

————. *Gradual Economic Reform in Latin America: The Costa Rican Experience.* Albany: State University of New York Press, 2001.

Clifton, Julian and Angela Benson. "Planning for Sustainable Ecotourism: The Case for Research Ecotourism in Developing Country Destinations." *Journal of Sustainable Tourism 14* (2006): 238-54.

Coaliciòn Costarricense de Iniciativas para el Desarrollo, accessed March 9, 2011, http://www.cinde.org.

Coone, Tim. "Costa Rica's 'eco-tourism' helps precious rain forests." *The Financial Post* (Canada), November 13, 1989.

Cottrell, Stuart , Rene van der Duim, Patricia Ankersmid and Liesbeth Kelder. "Measuring the Sustainability of Tourism in Manuel Antonio and Texel: A Tourist Perspective." *Journal of Sustainable Tourism 12* (2004): 409-31.

Cruz, Consuelo. "Identity and Persuasion. How nations remember their pasts and make their futures." *World Politics 52* (2000): 275-312.

Cusack, Daniela and Lydia Dixon. "Community-Based Ecotourism and Sustainability: Cases in Bocas del Toro Province, Panama and Talamanca, Costa Rica." *Journal of Sustainable Forestry 22* (2006): 157-82.

Danse, Myrtille and Teun Wolters. "Sustainable Coffee in the Mainstream: The Case of the SUSCOF Consortium in Costa Rica." *Greener Management International 43* (2003): 37-51.

Dellaert, Benedict G. C. and Kreg Lindberg. "Variations in Tourist Price Sensitivity: A Stated Preference Model to Capture the Joint Impact of Differences in Systematic Utility and Response Consistency." *Leisure Sciences 25* (2003): 81-96.

Duffy, Rosaleen. "Neoliberalising Nature: Global Networks and Ecotourism Development in Madagascar." *Journal of Sustainable Tourism 16* (2008): 327-44.

Eade, Catherine. "Costa Rica? The perfect destination for adventure seekers, wildlife fans and lovers of rolling green hills—'pura vida' indeed." *Daily Mail (UK)*, January 6, 2011.

Environmental Performance Index, accessed December 21, 2011, http://epi. yale.edu/.

Epler Wood, Megan. "Ecotourism: Principles, Practices & Policies for Sustainability." Paris: United Nations Environmental Program. 2002.

Evans, Sterling. *The Green Republic: A Conservation History of Costa Rica.* Austin: University of Texas Press, 1999.

Food and Agricultural Organization of the United Nations. "The WTO Agreement on Agriculture: The Implementation Experience-Developing Country Case Studies." Accessed January 5, 2010, http://www.fao.org/DOCREP/005/Y4632E/y4632e0a. htm#bm10.

Frank, David John. "Science, Nature, and the Globalization of the Environment, 1870-1990." *Social Forces 76* (1997): 409-35.

———, Ann Hironaka and Evan Schofer. "The Nation-State and the Natural Environment over the Twentieth Century." *American Sociological Review 65* (2000): 96-116.

Garcia-Barrios, Luis, Yankuic M. Galvan-Miyoshi, Valdivieso-Perez, Ingrid Abril, Omar R. Masera, Gerrado Bocco and John Vandermeer. "Neotropical Forest Conservation, Agricultural Intensification, and Rural Out-migration: The Mexican Experience." *BioScience 29* (2009): 863-73.

Geldermann, U. and K-H Kogel. "Nature's Concept. The 'New Agriculture' amidst Ecology, Economy, and the Demythologization of the Gene." *Journal of Agronomy and Crop Science 188* (2002): 368-75.

Giannecchini, Joan. "Ecotourism: New Partners. New Relationships." *Conservation Biology 7*, (1993): 429-32.

Gibson, Charles. *Tlaxcala in the Sixteenth Century.* Stanford: Stanford University Press, 1993.

Gindling, T. H. "South-South Migration: The Impact of Nicaraguan Immigrants on Earnings, Inequality and Poverty in Costa Rica." *World Development 37* (2009): 116-26.

Gudmundson, Lowell. *Costa Rica Before Coffee: Society and Economy on the Eve of the Export Boom.* Baton Rouge: Louisiana State University Press. 1986.

Guess, George M. "Pasture Expansion, Forestry, and Development Contradictions: The Case of Costa Rica." *Studies in Comparative International Development 14* (1979): 42-55.

Hanna, Rosine and Tugrul U. Daim. "Managing offshore outsourcing in the software industry." *Technology Analysis and Strategic Management 21* (2009): 881-97.

Happy Planet Index, accessed August 21, 2010, www.happyplanetindex.org.

Harrison, Lawrence H. *Underdevelopment Is a State of Mind.* Boston: The Center for International Affairs, Harvard University and University Press of America, 1985.

Hawkins, Donald E. "A Protected Areas' Ecotourism Competitive Cluster Approach to Catalyse Biodiversity Conservation and Economic Growth in Bulgaria." *Journal of Sustainable Tourism 12* (2004): 219-44.

Hazbun, Waleed. *Beaches, Ruins, and Resorts: The Politics of Tourism in the Arab World.* Minneapolis: University of Minnesota Press, 2008.

Homer-Dixon, Thomas. "The Ingenuity Gap: Can Poor Countries Adapt to Resource Scarcity?" *Population and Development Review 21* (1995): 587-612.

Honey, Martha. *Ecotourism and Sustainable Development: Who Owns Paradise?* Second Edition. Washington: Island Press, 2008.

———. "Spectrum: Buying peace with a park—Conservation is not only helping end war in Central America but is also cutting Costa Rica's huge foreign debt." *The Times* (London), February 10, 1988.

———. "Giving a Grade to Costa Rica's Green Tourism." *NACLA Report on the Americas XXXVI.* (2003): 39-47.

Huntington, Samuel P. *Political Order in Changing Societies.* New Haven: Yale University Press, 1968.

Instituto Costarricense de Turismo, accessed March 12, 2012, http://www.visitcosta rica.com.

Instituto Nacional de Aprendizaje, accessed July 30, 2009, http:://www.ina.ac.cr.

Inter-American Development Bank. "Costa Rica: IDB Country Strategy with Costa Rica, 2006-2010," 2007.

International Coffee Organization, accessed March 21, 2009, http://www. ico.org.

International Ecotourism Society. "What Is Ecotourism?" accessed October 27, 2011, http://www.ecotourism.org.

Juan, Stephen, "Costa Rica Invests in Its People; Only Human." *Sydney Morning Herald.* (Australia), August 25, 1988.

Keitumetse, S.O. "The Eco-tourism of Cultural Heritage Management (ECT-CHM): Linking Heritage and 'Environment' in the Okavango Delta Regions of Botswana." *International Journal of Heritage Studies* 15 (2009): 223-44.

Koens, Jacobus Franciscus, Carol Dieperink, and Miriam Miranda. "Ecotourism as development strategy: Experiences from Costa Rica." *Environment, Development, and Sustainability 11* (2009): 1225-37.

Konadu-Agyemang, Kwadwo. "Structural adjustment programmes and the international tourism trade in Ghana: Some socio-spatial implications." *Tourism Geographies 3* (2001): 187-206.

Kramer, Wendy. *Encomienda Politics in Early Colonial Guatemala 1524-1544. Dividing the Spoils.* Boulder: Westview Press, 1994.

Langholz, Jeff, James Lassoie, and John Schelhas. "Incentives for Biological Conservation: Costa Rica's Private Wildlife Refuge Program." *Conservation Biology 14* (2000): 1735-43.

Lehoucq, Fabrice Edouard. *Instituciones democraticas y conflictos politicos en Costa Rica.* Heredia: Editorial UNA, 1998.

Locke, Steven. "Environmental education for democracy and social justice in Costa Rica." *International Research in Geographical and Environmental Education. 18* (2009), 97-110.

Longo, Stefano and Richard York. "Agricultural Exports and the Environment: A Cross-National Study of Fertilizer and Pesticide Consumption." *Rural Sociology 73:* (2008) 82-104.

Loveman, Brian. *The Constitution of Tyranny: Regimes of Exception in Spanish America.* Pittsburgh: University of Pittsburgh Press, 1993.

MacLeod, Donald V. L. "Tourism and the Globalization of a Canary Island." *The Journal of the Royal Anthropological Institute 5* (1999): 443-56.

Magnotta, Vince and Ann Magnotta. "Costa Rica's Literacy Boom." *The Christian Science Monitor.* 31, November 4. 1985.

Mahoney, James. "Radical, Reformist and Aborted Liberalism: Origins of National Regimes in Central America. *Journal of Latin American Studies 33* (2001) 221-56.

Mandelbaum, Michael. *The Ideas that Conquered the World: Peace, Democracy, and Free Markets in the 21ˢᵗ Century.* New York: Public Affairs, 2002.

Marquette, Catherine M. "Nicaraguan Migrants in Costa Rica." *Poblacion y Salud en Mesoamerica 4* (2006).

Matarrita-Cascante, David, Mark Anthony Brennan and A. E. Luloff. "Community Agency and Sustainable Tourism Development: The Case of La Fortuna, Costa Rica." *Journal of Sustainable Tourism 18* (2010): 735-56.

McCreery, David J. *The Sweat of Their Brow: A History of Work in Latin America.* Armonk: M.E. Sharpe, 2000.

Ministerio de Educacion Publica de la Republica de Costa Rica. *Programas de Ingles III Ciclo,* accessed December 21, 2008, http://www.mep.go.cr/.

Monge Alfaro, Carlos. *Historia de Costa Rica.* San José: Imprenta Trejos, 1980.

Moon Travel Guide. "Costa Rica's Oscar Arias Administration Pulling Down Hotels," accessed August 1, 2011, http://www.moon.com/print/85381.

Morales, Luis and Lawrence Pratt. *Analysis of the Daniel Oduber Quiros International Airport, Liberia Costa Rica.* San José: Center for Responsible Travel, 2010.

Moreno, Peter S. "Ecotourism Along the Meso-American Caribbean Reef: The Impacts of Foreign Investment." *Human Ecology 33* (2005): 217-44.

Morley, Samuel A. *Poverty and Inequality in Latin America: The Impact of Adjustment and Recovery in the 1980s.* Baltimore: Johns Hopkins University Press, 1995.

Mowforth, Martin and Ian Munt. *Tourism and Sustainability: Development, Globalization, and New Tourism in the Third World.* Third Edition. London: Routledge, 2009.

Mycoo, Michelle. "Sustainable Tourism Using Regulations, Market Mechanisms and Green Certification: A Case Study of Barbados." *Journal of Sustainable Tourism 14* (2006):489-511.

National System of Conservation Areas, accessed August 4, 2011, http://www. costarica-nationalparks.com/.

The Nature Conservancy, accessed October 23, 2010, http://www.nature.org.

Nelson, Roy C. "Competing for Foreign Direct Investment: Efforts to Promote Non-traditional FDI in Costa Rica, Brazil, and Chile." *Studies in Comparative International Development 40* (2005): 3-28.

———. *Harnessing Globalization: The Promotion of Nontraditional Foreign Direct Investment in Latin America.* University Park: The Pennsylvania State University Press, 2009.

Nemasetoni, Irene and Christian M. Rogerson. "Developing Small Firms in Township Tourism: Emerging Tour Operators in Gauteng, South Africa." *Urban Form 16* (2005): 196-213.

Nomura, Ko, Latipah Hendarti and Osamu Abe. "NGO Environmental Education Centers in Developing Countries: Role, Significance and Keys to Success, from a "Change Agent" Perspective." *International Review for Environmental Strategies 4* (2003): 165-82

Orams, Mark B. "The Effectiveness of Environmental Education: Can We Turn Tourists into 'Greenies'? *Progress in Tourism and Hospitality Research 3* (1997): 295-306.

Organization for Economic Co-Operation and Development. 2003. "Caribbean Rim Investment Initiative Business Environment Report Costa Rica, April 20, 2003.

Ormsby, Alison and Kathryn Mannle. "Ecotourism Benefits and the Role of Local Guides at Masoala National Park, Madagascar." *Journal of Sustainable Tourism 14* (2006): 271-87.

Overseas Security Advisory Council. "Costa Rica 2010 Crime & Safety Report. Accessed September 1, 2011, http://www.osac.org.

Paarlberg, Robert. "The Ethics of Modern Agriculture." *Society 46* (2009): 4-8.

Paige, Jeffrey M. *Coffee and Power: Revolution and the Rise of Democracy in Central America.* Cambridge: Harvard University Press, 1997.

Paus, Eva A. *Foreign Investment, Development, and Globalization: Can Costa Rica Become Ireland?* New York: Palgrave MacMillan, 2005.

Peake, Sheila. Peter Innes, and Pam Dyer. "Ecotourism and Conservation: Factors influencing effective conservation messages." *Journal of Sustainable Tourism 17* (2009): 107-27.

Pendergrast, Mark. *Uncommon Grounds: The History of Coffee and How It Transformed the World.* New York: Basic Books, 1999.

Place. Susan E. "The Impact of National Park Development on Tortuguero, Costa Rica." *Journal of Cultural Geography 9* (1999): 37-53.

Prasso, Sheridan. "The Best Places to Vacation. (Where the Dollar Is Actually Worth Something) *Money 37* (2008): 122.

PROCOMER. The Foreign Trade Corporation of Costa Rica, accessed December 21, 2008, http://www.procomer.com.

Quesada, Gabriel A. "Garantías Ambientales en la Constitución: Un nuevo modelo ecológico-politico para *Costa Rica* y el resto del mundo." *Revista de Biologia Tropical 57,* (2009): 461-72.

Quiros, Claudia. "Hunting Indians." Pp. 16-21, in *The Costa Rica Reader: History, Culture, Politics*, edited by Steven Palmer and Ivan Molina. 16-21. Durham: Duke University Press, 2004.

Rain Forest Alliance. 2000. "Mohonk Agreement: Proposal for an International Certification Program for Sustainable Tourism and Ecotourism." Accessed July 7, 2011, http://www. rainforest-alliance.org/tourism/documents/mo honk. pdf.

Ramirez, Alonso. "Ecological Research and the Costa Rican Park System." *Ecological Applications 14* (2004): 25-27.

Reilly, William K. "Debt-for-Nature Swaps: The Time Has Come." *International Environmental Affairs 2* (1990): 134-40.

Reyes, Javier A. and W. Charles Sawyer. *Latin American Economic Development.* London: Routledge, 2011.

Rivera, Jorge. "Assessing a voluntary environmental initiative in the developing world: The Costa Rican Certification for Sustainable Tourism." *Policy Studies 35* (2003): 333-60.

———— and Peter De Leon. "Chief Executive Officers and voluntary environmental performance: Costa Rica's certification for sustainable tourism." *Policy Sciences 38* (2005): 107-27.

Rodriguez-Clare, Andres. "Costa Rica's Development Strategy based on Human Capital and Technology: How it got there, the impact of Intel, and lessons for other countries." *Journal of Human Development 2* (2001): 311-24.

Rodriguez-Saenz, Eugenia. "Relaciones Ilicitas y Matrimonios Desiguales. Pp. 185-210, in *Politics, Economy, and Society in Bourbon Central America, 1759-1821*, edited by Jordana Dym and Christophe Belaubre. Boulder: University Press of Colorado, 2007.

Rolla San Francisco, Andrea, Melissa Arias and Renata Villers. "Quality early childhood education in Costa Rica? Policy, practice, outcomes and challenges." *Early Years 25* (2005): 113-27.

Rutagarama, Eugene and Adrian Smith. "Partnerships for Protected Area Conservation in Rwanda." *The Geographical Journal 172* (2006): 291-305.

Sandoval-Garcia, Carlos. *Threatening Others: Nicaraguans and the Formation of National Identities in Costa Rica*. Athens: Ohio University Press, 2004.

Schendler, Auden. "Applying the Principle of Industrial Ecology to the Guest-Services Sector." *Journal of Industrial Ecology 7*, (2003): 127-38.

Schofer, Evan and Francisco J. Granados. "Environmentalism, Globalization and National Economies, 1980-2000." *Social Forces 85* (2006): 965-91.

Schwab, Klaus. "The Global Competitiveness Report: 2009-2010." Geneva: World Economic Forum, 2009.

Seligson, Mitchell A. *Peasants of Costa Rica and the Development of Agrarian Capitalism*. Madison: University of Wisconsin Press, 1980.

———— and Juliana Martinez Franzoni. "Limits to Costa Rican Heterodoxy: What Has Changed in "Paradise?" Pp. 307-37, in *Democratic Governance in Latin America*, edited by Scott Mainwaring and Timothy R. Scully. Stanford: Stanford University Press, 2010.

Selvatura Park, accessed July 12, 2011, http://selvatura.com.

Sherman, William L. *Forced Native Labor in Sixteenth-Century Central America*. Lincoln: University of Nebraska Press, 1979.

Sick, Deborah. "Coping with Crisis: Costa Rican Households and the International Coffee Market. *Ethnology 36* (1997): 255-75.

————. "Coffee, Farming Families, and Fair Trade in Costa Rica." *Latin American Research Review 43* (2008): 193-208.

Silva, Eduardo. "Sustainable Development and Shortchanging Social Ecology in Costa Rican Forest Policy." *Latin American Politics and Society 45*, (2003): 93-127.

Skidmore, Thomas E. and Peter H. Smith. *Modern Latin America*. New York: Oxford University Press, 2003.

Spar, Deborah. "Attracting high technology investment: Intel's Costa Rica plant." FIAS Occasional Paper 11, World Bank, Washington, D.C., 1998.

Stem, Caroline J., James P. Lassoie, David R. Lee, David D. Deshler, and John W. Schelhas. "Community Participation in Ecotourism Benefits: The Link to Conservation Practices and Perspectives. *Society and Natural Resources 16* (2003): 387-413.

Stone, Samuel. *La Dinastia de Conquistadores: La Crises del Poder en la Costa Rica Contemporanea*. San José: Editorial Universitaria Centroamericana, 2003.

Tamborini, Christopher R. "Work, Wages and Gender in Export-Oriented Cities: Global Assembly versus International Tourism in Mexico." *Bulletin of Latin America Research 26* (2007): 24-49.

Torres, Rebecca. "Toward a better understanding of tourism and agricultural linkages in the Yucatan: Tourist food consumption and preferences." *Tourism Geographies 4* (2002): 282-306.

———. "Gringolandia: The Construction of Tourist Space in Mexico." *Annals of the American Association of American Geographers 95* (2005); 314-35.

Tripathi, Shalini N. and Masood H. Siddiqui. "An empirical study of tourist preferences using conjoint analysis." *International Journal of Business Science and Applied Management 5* (2010): 2-16.

United Nations Environmental Programme. "Towards a Green Economy: Pathways to Sustainable Development and Poverty Eradication." Accessed January 5, 2012, www.unep.org/greeneconomy.

United Nations Office on Drugs and Crime. "Crime and Development in Central America." Accessed March 14, 2012, http://www.unodc.org/pdf/research/central_america_ study.pdf.

U.S. Department of State. "Travel Advisory Mexico." Accessed April 23, 2012, http://www. travel.state.gov/travel/cis_pa_tw/tw/tw_4755.html.

Vivanco, Luis A. "Spectacular Quetzals, Ecotourism, and Environmental Futures in Monte Verde, Costa Rica." *Ethnology 40* (2001): 79-92.

Wall, Geoffrey and Alistair Mathieson. *Tourism: Change, Impacts and Opportunities.* Harlow: Pearson Education Limited, 2006.

Wallace, David Rains. *The Quetzal and the Macaw: The Story of Costa Rica's National Parks.* San Francisco: Sierra Club Books. 1992.

Weinberg, Adam, Story Bellows. and Dara Ekster, "Sustaining Ecotourism: Insights and Implications from Two Successful Case Studies." *Society and Natural Resources 15* (2002) 371-80.

Wesson, Robert. *Democracy in Latin America: Promise and Problems.* New York: Praeger, 1982.

Williams, Adam. "New Costa Rica tourism campaign promotes 'pura vida' in US." *The Tico Times,* January 28, 2011.

———. "Hotel Closings on Costa Rica's Caribbean Coast spark violence." *The Tico Times,* July 29, 2011

Williams, Densil A. and Derrick Deslandes. "Motivation for Service Sector Foreign Direct Investments in Emerging Economies: Insights from the Tourism Industry in Jamaica." *The Round Table* 97, (2008): 419-37.

Wilson, Bruce M. *Costa Rica: Politics, Economics, and Democracy.* Boulder: Lynne Rienner Publishers, 1998.

World Bank. "World Bank Economic Indicators" Accessed April 23, 2011. http://data.worldbank.org/data-catalog/world-development-indicators.

———. "Costa Rica Country Economic Memorandum: The Challenges for Sustained Growth." Poverty Reduction and Economic Management Sector Unit Report #36180-CR, September 20, 2006.

———. "The Impact of Intel in Costa Rica: Nice Years after the Decision to Invest." Investing in Development Series, May 2006.

Xu, Jianying, Yihe Lu, Liding Chen and Yang Liu. "Contribution of tourism development to protected area management: Local stakeholder perspectives." *International Journal of Sustainability Development and World Ecology 16,* (2010): 30-36.

Yashar, Deborah J. *Demanding Democracy: Reform and Reaction in Costa Rica and Guatemala.* Stanford: Stanford University Press, 1997.

Yeager, Timothy J. "Encomienda or Slavery? The Spanish Crown's Choice of Labor Organization in Sixteenth-Century Spanish America." *The Journal of Economic History 55.* (1995): 842-59.

Zanotti, Laura and Janet Chernela. "Conflicting Cultures of Nature: Ecotourism, Education and the Kayapo of the Brazilian Amazon." *Tourism Geographies 10,* (2008): 495-521.

Zografos, Christos and David Allcroft. "The Environmental Values of Potential Ecotourists: A Segmentation Study. *Journal of Sustainable Tourism 15,* (2007): 44-66.

Index